DATE			
JUL 6 '93			
AUG 1 3 '93			
SEP 1 0 '93			
NOV 1 7 '93			
JAN 1 1 '94			
MAR 1 6 '94			
APR 1 3 '94			
APR 2 6 '94			
JUN 2 3 '94			
JUL 2 1 '94			
JUN 7 '9			

Magic Kingdoms

DISCOVERING THE JOYS OF
CHILDHOOD CLASSICS WITH YOUR CHILD

by Regina Higgins

SIMON & SCHUSTER
New York London Toronto Sydney Tokyo Singapore

SIMON & SCHUSTER
Simon & Schuster Building
Rockefeller Center
1230 Avenue of the Americas
New York, New York 10020

SIMON & SCHUSTER and colophon are registered trademarks of
Simon & Schuster Inc.

Designed by Karolina Harris
Manufactured in the United States of America

1   3   5   7   9   10   8   6   4   2

Library of Congress Cataloging-in-Publication Data

Higgins, Regina.
Magic kingdoms : discovering the joys of childhood classics with
your child / by Regina Higgins.
p.   cm.
Includes index.
1. Children's stories, English—History and criticism.
2. Children's stories, American—History and criticism.
3. Children—Books and reading.   4. Canon (Literature)   I. Title.
PR830.C513H54   1992
820.9′9282—dc20   92-15088   CIP
ISBN 0-671-73596-9

ACKNOWLEDGMENTS

FROM the beginning, I wanted this book to be a help to parents in understanding a shared concern: the growth of our children through reading. As I wrote the book, many parents and teachers shared their ideas and memories of childhood reading with me, and I'm especially grateful to Laura Bonde, Mara Lea Rosenbarger, Laura Dawkins, Taufiq Rashid, Debbi Edelstein, Karla Johnson, Stewart Roberts, Bridget Lynch, Jim Stark, Risë Paynter, Joby Copenhaver, and Valerie Long.

It was in college that I first read Joseph Campbell's *The Hero with a Thousand Faces,* and his idea of the "monomyth" has inspired my own understanding of the magic kingdom. And like everyone writing about British children's literature, I've learned much from the books of Humphrey Carpenter, Martin Gardner, Roger Sale, Alison Lurie, and many other scholars. In particular, Carpenter's *Secret Gardens: The Golden Age of Children's Literature* offers a wealth of biographical detail, while Andrew Birkin's *J. M. Barrie and the Lost Boys* and Christopher Milne's *The Enchanted Places* afford a close view of the family life of two important authors in a way that touches the heart.

I'm grateful to my editor at Simon & Schuster, Bob Bender, and to my agent, John Ware, for their consistent help and encouragement. My thanks also to assistant editor Johanna Li, production editor Gypsy da Silva, and designer Karolina Harris.

And, of course, special thanks go to my husband, Charles, and to our daughter, Franny. It is their wisdom and imagination that have taught me most about the magic kingdom.

Bloomington, Indiana   REGINA HIGGINS
April 1992

This book is dedicated to your child
and to the child in you.

CONTENTS

CHAPTER ONE

The Magic Kingdom of Childhood

I was in the bookstore on a busy Saturday morning, looking for a special gift. A friend from college, a new mother, had written me a light-hearted account of life with the baby and had mentioned that she was planning to gather a small library for her child to grow into as the years passed, just as I'd done for my daughter, Franny. It was early yet, she knew, but did I have any suggestions about books for children?

The idea of a growing library for a growing child delighted me, and I was determined to make a contribution as well as some suggestions. From my own experience with Franny, I knew that an essential part of the magic of reading is contained in the shared book itself, an endearing, familiar expression of the love between parent and child. Opened thousands of times, paged through again and again with excitement, a special book bears the unmistakable signs of the delight of exploring together. A loved book, like a teddy bear, shows its wear to advantage. The more handled and worn it becomes, the greater its value.

To offer a book to a child is to offer a world to explore. It is in books, after all, that we first come to discover ourselves in self-consciousness. When you open a book for your child and share it in reading, you're giving shape and dimension to the routine events of everyday life, making it possible for your child to discover the meaning of childhood itself.

But what kind of childhood will your child discover? That depends almost entirely on the book you choose to offer. It is only in certain special books that you'll find a childhood worthy of the name, one that you can share and enjoy together and pass along, too. These are the books that can make a favorite toy as full of life as Winnie-the-Pooh, turn a backyard into Wonderland, or a porch into Captain Hook's pirate ship. They are the books that place your child at the center of the world of imagination, where childhood and adolescence can mean adventure and growth, and where growing up is the ultimate adventure. These are the books that will make your child the hero of his own childhood and ruler of a magic kingdom.

IN the bookstore's newly expanded children's section, I picked up Lewis Carroll's *Alice's Adventures in Wonderland*. I opened it and saw Alice standing quietly, like me, only instead of a row of books she was contemplating the huge, grinning Cheshire Cat in a tree. I was impressed by the calm assurance of her stance, nothing less than admirable, considering her circumstances. Here was a child who was adventurous and unafraid and even modest about it. In her story, she was the ruler—not the victim—of power.

My mind was made up. *Alice* in hand, I walked to the register at the front of the bookstore, remembering how I had recently read aloud the tales of Wonderland and the Looking-Glass World with my daughter, and how together we cheered our heroine on through the mazes of mirrors and dreams as she came to realize that she was the true queen of her magic kingdom. When I was a child, I remembered as I read to Franny, I wished to be like Alice—courageous, unflappable—the girl who always knew which way was up, even down a rabbit-hole.

And in sharing Alice's adventures with Franny, I had felt as if I were re-creating for her a special world of the imagination that I myself had explored as a child. Alice's triumphs had once been mine; now they were Franny's, too. This was the vision of childhood—and of parenthood—that I wanted to pass along to my friend and her newborn baby.

OF all the privileges of adulthood, surely one of the sweetest is the pleasure—indeed, the honor—of opening the door to the magic kingdom of imagination and fantasy for children. Of course, from the beginning, you want to read all sorts of books and stories to your child, just as later you'll want him

[13]

to choose to read a wide selection of literature on his own. But there are certain special books that we all enjoyed as young readers that we now look forward to sharing with our children, magic kingdoms of the imagination where they can discover fun and adventure and heroism in childhood.

When parents ask me which books they should read to their children for enjoyment and, increasingly, to provide a head start on cultural literacy, I begin by asking them which books they enjoyed when they were growing up. No one, it seems, can talk about the books they loved as children without smiling. *Alice's Adventures in Wonderland. Winnie-the-Pooh. Peter Pan. The Wind in the Willows.* The *Narnia* books. *The Lord of the Rings. The Wonderful Wizard of Oz.* The titles themselves conjure up a magic that wraps us in a memory of childhood.

All these books hold much more than stories, we remember, for each offers a magic kingdom, an imaginary land created by an adult and given to a child to enjoy and to rule. From Wonderland and the Hundred Acre Wood, through the River Bank and Neverland, to Narnia and Middle-earth, our children discover magic kingdoms complete with secret gardens and secret languages, where they can grow and learn by living out their hopes and facing down their fears. And though these imaginary lands are all different and original, each of them representing a turning point in childhood, one magic kingdom leads inevitably to another, for part of the magic lies in the way your child will find them precisely when he needs them.

In reading these books to our sons and daughters, in encouraging them to read the stories for themselves, we help them to discover their own imaginations by introducing them to a common language and landscape of childhood that encompasses not only Wonderland and Neverland but the Land of Oz and even Disneyland. And it's your child's fluency in this language, his innate sense of direction in the magic kingdom, that enables him to make the connection between his own imaginative growth and our shared sense of

[14]

the world around us. That is the beginning of cultural literacy in its truest form.

These stories define a tradition of childhood classics, and in a larger sense, childhood itself. In the collective world of the imagination that these books evoke, in the abiding vision of childhood that remains for all of us, your child will find the wide, welcoming woods beyond Christopher Robin's country house, and a nanny named Mary Poppins who carries magic in her umbrella. And here your child will meet a rabbit who doesn't merely talk about being late, but consults a pocketwatch that he tucks inside his waistcoat pocket, like any properly dressed gentleman in Oxford's High Street. A favorite memory for us and an adventure for our children, these stories of the magic kingdom seem part of a childhood dream we share, because they all come from the childhood of the modern world, when life began to take on the shape we recognize now.

THESE classics are the treasures of the "Golden Age" of childhood literature, roughly from the 1850s to the 1930s, when children's books in English acquired a depth and beauty that made them immortal as well as popular. We now think of Victorian London, that imperial city of hansom cabs and streets lit by gaslight, as an imaginary world in itself, a fitting time and place for the birth of a magic kingdom. In the 1950s when he was writing *The Chronicles of Narnia*, C. S. Lewis acknowledged his nostalgia for this "Golden Age" by setting *The Magician's Nephew*, the story of the creation of his own magic kingdom, in the 1890s—when "Mr. Sherlock Holmes was still living in Baker Street."

Appropriately, this tradition of the magic kingdom—these stories of children growing up in imagination—came from the time in history when Britain itself was growing up into an Empire and taking on the responsibilities of an international power. Over the course of a few generations, beginning in the 1850s, the British world grew larger, and British influence and duties immeasurably greater. In this period, at the pinnacle of its Empire, Britain held sway over fully one-quarter of the world's population, and in Parliament, the debating and voting affected life not just in Birmingham, but in Bombay, too.

At the time when these children's classics of the magic kingdom were written, all the centers of English power and culture, from the lecture halls of Oxford to the offices of *Punch,* were united in a spirit of noble purpose: to rule well and wisely a far-flung Empire, and to instruct an imperial people through intellect and imagination. This was the work to which the artists and writers of these books devoted themselves daily, and the classics they created on their own time, for children they loved, expressed this high purpose, the same idealism.

Not surprisingly, perhaps, the creators of this rich tradition of magic kingdoms were not primarily "children's" writers and artists. For the most part, they held important positions in prestigious places. Lewis Carroll dreamed of Wonderland while teaching at Oxford, where both C. S. Lewis and J. R. R. Tolkien would later write of Narnia and Middle-earth. J. M. Barrie, who wrote *Peter Pan,* was celebrated as a West End playwright of sophisticated, modern wit, on a par with George Bernard Shaw. The author of *The Wind in the Willows,* Kenneth Grahame, worked at the Bank of England in the 1890s, when that institution was not merely at the center of British finance, but the center of all world finance. Sir John Tenniel, the illustrator of Wonderland and the Looking-Glass World, as well as A. A. Milne and E. H. Shepard, who together produced the *Pooh* books, were on the staff of *Punch,* at that time the most influential political and humor magazine in the world.

As an illustration of the connection between imperial power and the magic kingdom, Tenniel's White Queen in Lewis Carroll's *Through the Looking-Glass* showed a remarkable resemblance to Queen Victoria herself, who was, in fact, known as the "White Queen" in many parts of the Empire.

Crowned when she was only eighteen, Victoria had been hailed by the *Times* of London as the "girl–Queen," and went on to reign for over sixty years, longer than any other British monarch. She not only defined her age but, quite literally, gave it a name.

Had Tenniel's illustration of the White Queen appeared in *Punch,* readers would have called it political satire, but in the magic kingdom of the Looking-Glass World it served a quite different purpose. For it is finally Alice who realizes the promise of the "girl–Queen." In fact, through her many adventures in Wonderland and the Looking-Glass World, including her own coronation in the magic kingdom, Queen Alice always demonstrates the royal virtues of the young Victoria—decisiveness, good sense, courage—a fact which Tenniel consciously underscores by twice flanking her with the Queen's most famous prime ministers, Gladstone and Disraeli.

In *Alice,* then, as in all the books of the magic kingdom, your child is offered a vision of the power of leadership and hope for youth discovering that power within itself. All these classics invite your child to see himself in the main character's place, gaining and ruling a magic kingdom with wisdom and benevolence. It's no wonder, then, that the worlds of these classic stories bear a distinct family resemblance, and that one seems inevitably to lead to another.

CHILDREN enjoy characters they can identify with, and they also love the idea of creating an entire world, populating it with strange creatures, and setting it in motion. For your child, this is where the familiar and the fantastic can meet on equal terms, where time stands still or follows its own rules, where to believe six impossible things before breakfast is a royal virtue.

There is indeed a magical enchantment to an imaginary land, a place your child can enter only through a special book to discover the essential geography of childhood. You start your child on this imaginative journey when you put your arm around her and open the world before you both by opening the covers of a book. For a book *is* a world, one in which you and your child can share an imaginative life together. And the adventures you embark on are a way of becoming closer, of sharing a vision of childhood that opens possibilities for the future.

When you sit your child on your lap and open A. A. Milne's *Winnie-the-Pooh,* for example, you discover together a land of the imagination already mapped out for you. With its scrawled legend, "Drawn by Me and Mr Shepard Helpd," the two-page map is, like a child, at once engagingly exact and abstract, showing indications for "My House" and "Pooh Bears House"—these two most important places in big, bold letters—as well as the "100 Aker Wood" and the enchanted place where Pooh and his companion will at last part, but now marked only with the helpful notation "Nice for Piknicks."

For you, one look at this pictorial table of contents can bring back the adventures of Christopher Robin, Pooh, Piglet, and the rest, because each story is, in some way, reflected in the landscape of your own childhood reading. Here is "Where the Woozle Wasnt," near the "Floody Place" where Pooh rescues Piglet. The "Pooh Trap for Heffalumps," you show your child, lies on the opposite side of "Owls House" from "Eeyores Gloomy Place," which is appropriately "Rather Boggy and Sad."

Your child will notice the tiny dots throughout the map, and will perhaps trace them with a finger. They mark the paths from one character to another, from place to place, promising exciting possibilities, and ultimately charting Christopher Robin's growth from a child in the nursery to a boy in the schoolroom. And should your child wonder where this particular imaginary land lies, you can find a gentle reminder in the upper left corner of the map, where the compass, neatly drawn, points out the four corners of Christopher Robin's magic kingdom: P-O-O-H.

[18]

This practice of plotting out an imaginary landscape on a map—as if it all actually existed alongside every other place you know—makes it more real and more fantastic at the same time. And, of course, "Where the Woozle Wasnt" is only the beginning. You and your child still have directions to follow like Peter Pan's "second to the right and straight on till morning," landmarks to scout like Toad Hall and the lamppost at the border of Narnia, and beyond that the vast kingdoms of Mordor and Westernesse charted out on Tolkien's elaborately detailed cosmological map of Middle-earth. All these and more are part of the magic that brings together "here" and "there" so beautifully and so memorably in a world of fantasy that you can share with your child. When you read these stories together, you're opening the door to the magic kingdom of childhood, encouraging your child to wander and play where you—where all of us—learned the wonder and happiness of imagination.

WHETHER in the Hundred Acre Wood, Wonderland, Neverland, or Middle-earth, from a world as small as a teddy bear to a realm as large as imagination itself, you and your child will find the same unchanging tale in a vision of growing independence and action. In all these classic stories a child unlocks an unknown world, explores it, finds it full of challenges, and, by dint of courage and right thinking, becomes that world's acknowledged ruler before returning to ordinary life.

The experience is temporary and fantastic, of course—sometimes it's a dream, sometimes not—but the effects, according to the story, are always permanent and real. In fact, your child can point out the changes realized by these adventures: Christopher Robin learns to read and write, Alice comes to rely on her own common sense, Wendy grows up while remaining young at heart. These children—and your child, too—are all wiser now, older somehow, and more sure of themselves, because of their experiences.

As you and your child read on, the challenges of the magic kingdom become increasingly more difficult. Christopher Robin must sort out the embarrassing dilemmas his bear finds himself in, Alice must stand up for her logical views all alone in the face of Wonderland's absurdity, Wendy struggles to keep the vital connection between Neverland and London, and Frodo answers the summons to undertake a perilous journey through right and wrong to save his world.

The stakes may change, but the magic endures. Again and again it summons your child away from everyday life into a secret world that demands involvement and growth, where fears are faced and hopes realized. Your child journeys with the children of these classic stories, living out their adventures and meeting their challenges in the magic kingdom of imagination that you've opened up together in the pages of a book.

This is reading at its best, active and engaging. And when you hold your child on your lap to read one of these very special books, you should know that you're not simply letting him retreat into fantasy so that he can make believe. You're preparing him to advance into reality so he can make a difference.

THIS tradition of best-loved books began in Victorian times, when parents believed, as we do now, that teaching children to do right would make a difference in the world. The age of action and optimism demanded children's stories that emphasized confidence and courage, and showed the benefits of being true to one's finest instincts.

The children of these stories, then, are thoroughly good-hearted and need only a challenge to reveal their best selves. Once they've accomplished this goal at the end of their journey, they come into what seems a natural inheritance: being crowned ruler of the magic kingdom, not so much as a conventional reward but as a natural acknowledgment of character.

In consequence, the realm of Narnia has been waiting for its rulers since the dawn of time, until Peter, Susan, Edmund, and Lucy find the secret passage to the Kingdom through the wardrobe in the spare room. Their mere presence, in fact, is a dire threat to the White Witch who holds Narnia in thrall. A prophecy foretells that when two Sons of Adam and two Daughters of Eve sit as kings and queens in Cair Paravel, the Witch's evil reign—and her life—will be over.

Even the mistakes the children make are part of the triumphal procession to their thrones, for it is Edmund's slip with the Turkish Delight that makes possible the Lion Aslan's noble sacrifice. When Aslan crowns all four children, it is not just for their valor in battle against the White Witch, although they've all played their parts with courage and honor. Their thrones have awaited them since the beginning of Narnia's history. The coronation dramatizes that the children have been and always will be the center of true power, and of meaning itself, in the kingdom of Narnia.

It is this unqualified reverence for childhood that makes the tale of Narnia so powerful and so memorable for us. And this affirming of a child's place in the world—indeed, at the very center of the world—is the hallmark of all these classics. Each of these special books glorifies a child who represents all children, and in doing so allows your child to enjoy through imagination the highest honor the magic kingdom has to offer.

THE first story of the magic kingdom began, appropriately, at a child's request, a magical, royal command. Alice Liddell, one of three daughters of a dean at Oxford, had been befriended by Charles Lutwidge Dodgson, a mathematics tutor at the college. Alice and her sisters frequently visited Dodgson at his rooms, begging him for stories, and, though he was quite shy and inclined to stammer before adults, he enjoyed improvising tales for his child-friends, sketching illustrations as he did so. It was a favorite joke among them that he would pretend to fall asleep in mid-story—much like the Dormouse in Wonderland—only to be awakened by the laughing sisters.

One afternoon in July of 1862, Dodgson, Alice, and her two sisters, along with Robinson Duckworth, a colleague of Dodgson's, set out on a boating expedition up the Thames from Oxford to Godstow for a picnic. Dodgson and Duckworth were both at the oars when Alice, seated in the prow, asked for a story. While rowing, Dodgson began telling a tale of a girl named Alice who pursued a rabbit down a hole and discovered an entire world—a magic kingdom—of fantastic creatures underground. Intrigued by what he was hearing, Duckworth turned abruptly around at his oars and interrupted Dodgson, wanting to know if he was actually making up this story as he was telling it. Yes, Dodgson assured him, he quite certainly was.

When they arrived back in Oxford late that evening, Alice begged Dodgson to write down the story for her, and the next day, on the morning train to London, he did write some notes, planning to call his tale "Alice's Adventures Underground." Eventually, as we all know, Dodgson's story became not one book but two—*Alice's Adventures in Wonderland* in 1865, followed by *Through the Looking-Glass* in 1871—both of them published under the pseudonym Lewis Carroll.

WHEN you and your child first open *Alice's Adventures in Wonderland,* you find together what Alice herself first sees—the White Rabbit consulting his pocketwatch. And thanks to Tenniel, there is wonderful attention to detail in the illustration here—the rabbit's precisely cut coat; his appropriately Victorian accoutrements, including the watch; even his portly dimensions that make the last button of his waistcoat strain dangerously, as if to pop—an elaboration of nuances reflecting the ordinary world. The only difference, of course, is that all this English conventionality holds a rabbit inside. And, as Alice later tells her sister, a talking rabbit is one thing, but a rabbit with a watch in his waistcoat is quite another.

Just like Alice, your child follows the White Rabbit into imagination, down the rabbit-hole and through the looking-glass into a fantasy world that's very much a model for all magic kingdoms. Made palpably real for your child by Tenniel's illustrations, it is in fact quite like Dodgson's own Victorian world—complete with a tea party, a game of croquet, a quadrille, poetry recitals, boating on a river, an elaborate dinner party, even a trial by jury and, of course, a coronation.

In the beginning, Alice simply wants to enter the secret garden she's discovered at the bottom of the rabbit-hole, but she can't because she never seems quite the right size. Confused, she even wonders if she's still the same person she was yesterday. She's always changing, but never comes any closer to what she wants or to feeling comfortable in her own body. At nine feet, she's crouching in a hall and trapped inside the White Rabbit's house. At a few inches, she's nearly drowning in the pool of tears she'd cried when she was taller. Of course, this is the uncomfortable dilemma every child faces, growing up and changing in ways that can't always be controlled or foreseen.

But through her adventures, Alice learns to take command of the situation and to stand up for herself. At the beginning of the chapter titled "A Mad Tea-Party," we see Alice seated in a thronelike chair, her eyes on the Mad Hatter, March Hare, and Dormouse. Her demeanor here expresses high—even royal—disapproval, and she seems, at this moment, ready to stand up and leave the party—as she does at the end of the chapter. This first image foreshadows her departure, so that when you read the account of all the contradictions and interruptions Alice suffers, your child knows even before you finish that Alice isn't going to be overcome by this mad—and maddening—group.

In Alice, your child discovers an ideal model, one who personifies the best qualities of discipline and freedom, and with her, enters a world that combines everyday life with the life of dreams. But it's not a "dream come true" in the ordinary sense, for the dreamworlds of Lewis Carroll aren't made to be merely observed and enjoyed. Like all magic kingdoms, these worlds require imaginative involvement from their readers, and more, they demand to be put in order—conquered, even—by a child.

AND so it is with Alice, her coronation the final proof of her intelligence, determination, and strength of character. At the heart of Lewis Carroll's magic kingdom, midway through the *Alice* books, your child finds the illustration of a chess game that opens *Through the Looking-Glass*. The caption here not only sums up the plot of the story as a chess problem, but also promises that Alice will indeed make her way as a pawn from one side of the board to the other: "White Pawn (Alice) to play, and win in eleven moves."

Like Shepard's map for the *Pooh* books, this chessboard is really a map of the Looking-Glass World, and the pieces on it are the characters. In the story itself, we follow Alice through various squares and see characters whose qualities are determined by their function in the chess game. The Queens move rapidly and freely, as queens really do in chess, while the Kings, like their chess counterparts, tend to remain still and apart from the action. Even the White Knight, with his clumsy, headlong falls from his halting mount, traces out the L-shaped move of this eccentric piece.

Many readers naturally associate the White Knight with Dodgson himself. At first, he seems to be simply an animated chess piece, but when he removes his helmet we see that he's very human, with a "gentle face and large, mild eyes." For all his harmless talk of misguided inventions and eccentric ideas, he's the only truly helpful and thoroughly likable character Alice meets in this magic kingdom. And it is the White Knight who escorts Alice safely to the Eighth Square and to queenhood, as she plays out her transition from pawn to queen to crown her growth from childhood toward adulthood.

According to the rules of chess, then, Alice realizes her

royal destiny and finally crosses into the Eighth Square—literally to be "queened." Jumping across the brook after the departure of the White Knight, she tumbles down into the soft grass, and suddenly senses something heavy around her head. And in this moment of magic coronation, Tenniel captures Alice as she first feels the golden crown upon her head—her face, in its only detailed study in the illustrations, radiant with wonder, an ineffable mixture of discovery and delight.

THE crowning may not always be as explicit as in *Alice* and *Narnia,* of course. The magic kingdom acknowledges the royalty of its child-adventurer in many ways. If Wendy isn't Queen of Neverland, she's certainly its Queen-Mother. Frodo has the chance to be Lord of Middle-earth, but refuses the dark throne for a hero's legacy. And although Christopher Robin is Good King Christopher only in Winnie-the-Pooh's dream, the boy takes it upon himself to knight his bear in royal fashion, with a twig from the Enchanted Place at the top of the Forest.

As it happens, Ashdown Forest—the "real" Forest, or the model for it—was the royal hunting ground of English kings in medieval and Renaissance times. In fact, in the year Christopher Robin Milne was nine, the people of Devonshire organized a pageant in celebration of their living piece of history. They invited their young neighbor, by then a literary celebrity by virtue of his father's books about him, to take part in "Ashdown Forest Through the Centuries," and he accepted gratefully. There was a solemn procession of knights at arms, Henry VIII and his courtiers hunting, witches being brought to trial, all representing the passing of the ages in the ancient wood. And out of the Forest at the end of the procession, with his bear and other toys, came Christopher Robin himself, the latest great historical figure the Forest had given the world.

At this point in the pageant, the boy carried his toys across a clearing and into the trees. This was the cue for actors costumed as Christopher Robin's famous toys to make their entrance. When the boy returned, Pooh Bear, Piglet and the rest were following him, as if suddenly magically alive. Christopher Robin and his friends sat in the grass surrounded by the trees of the Forest and had a picnic while the pageant figures filed slowly behind them. At the end of the line, Christopher Robin rose, and, gathering his friends around him, followed through the trees.

As an adult, Milne remembered the pageant with real pleasure, especially the implicit assumption that he—like Henry VIII—was part of history. In fact, his position in the pageant made it very clear that he was meant to represent not just part of history, but its triumphant culmination, the happy and innocent ending to all the medieval superstition and court intrigue. And when we imagine the scene ourselves, from the distance of more than fifty years, Christopher Robin in his crowning glory stands for all the children who have ever enjoyed the Pooh books—your own child most of all.

ALICE and Christopher Robin stand as the quintessential children of the magic kingdom, and not only because they're the first of their tradition. You don't have to be a girl to identify with Alice or a boy to want to be like Christopher Robin, because neither character is limited by someone's arbitrary idea of "girlhood" or "boyhood."

Both Alice and Christopher Robin are children capable of and interested in any number of experiences and kinds of play. For Alice, walking sedately in a garden comes naturally—and so does kicking a lizard up a chimney, if the need arises. Christopher Robin is ready to pull on his big boots and lead an expedition to the North Pole, but that doesn't mean he can't enjoy sitting by his bear to comfort him with a "sustaining" book.

Your child instinctively knows this, and can even explain it, if necessary. One afternoon during the spring my daughter Franny turned four, we went to the park and brought with us her own Pooh and assorted stuffed friends. Franny was gathering twigs in order to build a house for Eeyore when another child, a little older than she, came by and asked what she was doing. Franny told him, and, by way of explanation, added, "I'm Christopher Robin."

"But you can't be," the older child countered. "Christopher Robin is a boy."

"He's not a boy," said Franny with assurance, "he's a character."

And so he is. Anyone who opens the *Alice* or *Pooh* books is invited in, encouraged to imagine herself as the main character, and to enjoy the fun. At first, your baby delights in the pictures, watching the story unfold in images. Later, your child gazes into the world Tenniel and Shepard show us while you read the story to her. And soon she'll be taking the road to the land of imagination all by herself, understanding more and more with each reading that the greatest adventure is to be challenged by the world, and to act decisively to put it right.

Our best-loved classic stories, then, always acknowledge the child-hero, and allow him to enter an imaginative world where clear thinking, honesty, and independence make him the ruler of its magic kingdom. Through Christopher Robin and Alice and all the other young adventurers, your child becomes a conquering hero, too. And as you read with him the classic stories you remember and love, as you share with him this magic kingdom of the imagination, your child will come to discover himself as he really is—confident, courageous, and ready to make a difference in the world.

CHAPTER TWO

[Classics Illustrated]

THE picture of a young child with an open book on his lap is one of our fondest images of childhood. It's even more endearing, of course, when the child is *your* child, and the book one that you remember enjoying in the same way at the same age yourself, turning the pages slowly and telling the story over and over by looking at the pictures. For it is in the illustrations of best-loved books that your child first discovers the world of the imagination made real and comprehensible for him—a sustained vision that he can share with you and return to again and again.

It is these images that will make up his own growing imagination, its richness and quality determined by the pictures you choose. In a real sense, this is the beginning of cultural literacy, since every adult, we assume, should be able to recognize classic illustrations, like Tenniel's Alice or Shepard's Christopher Robin and Pooh. And most important, these classic illustrations reveal to your child the magic kingdom of childhood, an ideal world of shared cultural and social values that will remain with him into adulthood. These illustrations not only evoke the world of imagination but make it real—second nature, in fact—because it is introduced so early.

AT two and three years old, your child passes through a stage of intense visual acuity. Put simply, this means that she is probably capable of seeing even more in illustrations than you are, because the ability to devote absorbing attention to the world around us is one of the special attributes of early childhood.

In fact, Tenniel's illustrations of Alice capture exactly the sense of wonder in a child's expression as she encounters a new and strange world, whether she's confronted with a Cheshire Cat, or a caterpillar smoking a hookah atop a giant mushroom. But however strange the landscape or its characters become, Tenniel's drawings always show us clearly that Alice is neither taken in nor frightened by what she sees.

When you sit your child on your lap, then, and open up a book like *Alice* and show her the illustrations as you read, you're sharing with her a vision of childhood that will last a lifetime. Not only are you encouraging her to visualize the characters and scenes of the story, something all good readers do, you're also helping her to recognize the implicit connection between the pictures and the words as the images she sees and the words she hears come together effortlessly to create meaning.

By reading illustrated books with your child, you're building the groundwork for literacy in the most enjoyable way possible. Almost before she's begun, your child becomes confident about reading, and that confidence will carry her through many of the challenges in learning that lie ahead. She will also discover the source of her own imagination, that vital connection between the inner self and the landscape of childhood pictured for her in the pages of a book. This confidence, these discoveries, will prepare her for the adventure itself—her entrance into the magic kingdom and the glory of making it her own.

WORKING in this classic tradition today, Chris Van Allsburg brings to his illustrations the richness and wonder of the magic kingdom. With intensely realistic detail softened by shadow and light, Van Allsburg offers a landscape of memory and imagination, where a child travels, finds a treasure, and then returns to ordinary life. Perhaps the most appealing quality in Van Allsburg's work is its simplicity: the assertion that there is somehow a world of dreams where magic rules, and this is what it looks like.

For parents, Van Allsburg's illustrations recall a time when the world seemed much bigger and loomed around us like the arms of an overstuffed armchair. In gazing at the illustrations of *The Polar Express, Jumanji, Ben's Dream,* and *The Stranger,* adults regain their child-sight, while children find a door opened into a realm where dreams and reality exist together. And when the adventure is over and everything has returned to normal, there is always a small, unmistakable sign of some kind that it wasn't just a dream, that the mysterious world really does exist.

When Judy and Peter find the game Jumanji under a tree in the park and bring it home, they haven't any notion that they're about to enter another world with rules of its own. Although the Jumanji board game, which Van Allsburg shows us in an intriguing view from above, is simply a conventional, twisting path, like any other board game, the power it has when released by play is fantastic.

The object of the game is to reach Jumanji, the Golden City, and along the way are hazards and setbacks like "Lion attacks, move back two spaces" or "Monkeys steal food, miss one turn." The difference between Jumanji and any other typical board game is that the imaginary hazards become real—a lion suddenly appears, monkeys raid the kitchen—and the instructions clearly state that the game, once started, must be played to the end, until the Golden City is reached. Like Alice on the Looking-Glass chessboard, the children must face the challenges they meet until they reach the final square.

Judy and Peter roll the dice and move along the path, dodging a herd of rhinos and a python, amid monsoons and volcanoes, until, at last, the goal is reached and the game is won. Suddenly, the magic stops and the jungle hazards disappear. Relieved, the children quickly return the game to the park. Later that day, when they see two brothers carrying the game away, Judy and Peter wonder what will happen when the brothers release the power of Jumanji, especially if they fail to read the instructions before starting to play.

An image coming to life, becoming literally what it represents, is a favorite theme for Van Allsburg, and his illustrations capture the numinous quality of imagination. In his alphabet book, *The Z Was Zapped: A Play in Twenty-Six Acts,* letters themselves take on a wild, antic life of their own, in a fantasy that mimics reading. Open a book, open a game, Van Allsburg's pictures declare, and imagination can become reality.

But if this magic is to happen, it must be allowed to happen as it will. And it must be looked for, believed in, awaited with expectation, as we see in *The Polar Express.* On Christmas Eve, a boy lies in bed careful not to make a sound, listening with all his might for Santa's sleigh bells, despite his friend's insistence that there is no Santa. What he hears late that night draws him out of bed in curiosity and wonder— not the sound of sleigh bells, but a train that has screeched to a halt just outside his house. Before he knows it he's in his robe and slippers, walking outside, talking to a conductor, and boarding the Polar Express.

The ride to the North Pole, with passengers in pajamas, is a dream journey through snowy wilderness and mountains to the Great Polar Ice Cap and a city filled with toy factories. Here Santa will give the first gift of Christmas to one of the children on the train. When the boy is selected to ask Santa for the first gift, though he can have anything he imagines, he chooses a single silver bell from Santa's sleigh. Santa presents the gift to him and departs, sleigh bells ringing with the most beautiful sound the boy has ever heard. He puts his bell in the pocket of his robe and joins the other children for the train ride home.

On board the Polar Express, the boy discovers that the bell is gone, lost through a hole in his pocket. He returns sadly to bed, but on Christmas morning his little sister notices a small box with his name on it behind the tree. It is the bell Santa gave him, and attached is a note reading "Found this on the seat of my sleigh. Fix that hole in your pocket," and signed "Mr. C."

When he rings the bell, the boy and his sister listen with delight, but find to their surprise that their parents can't hear its sound. As the years pass, the friends who heard it that

[32]

Christmas—even the little sister—can't hear it any longer. The boy himself, the child who shook off disbelief, who listened closely and waited patiently on Christmas Eve, has grown old, but he tells us "the bell still rings for me as it does for all who truly believe."

In the last illustration we see the bell itself, luminously, almost photographically realistic, yet suffused with ineffable magic. It's a characteristic Van Allsburg illustration, haunting and evocative, returning to us something beautiful and extraordinary that we thought we'd lost forever. The image lingers in the memory, as classics do, remaining for us, and for all those who believe, a door into the past, to the magic kingdom of childhood.

JUST as Chris Van Allsburg's illustrations recall the golden age of our own childhood within the tradition of the magic kingdom, Beatrix Potter's popular tales open the door to an English country garden that remains a place of enchantment for all those who have visited there. Potter's little books were among the first I read to Franny, and they're a good place to start, not only because the stories themselves—about eating, escaping, working and playing—fascinate young children, but because Potter, as author and illustrator, offers a perfect, memorable combination of words and pictures. The tone of the stories seems made for a parent's voice—a unique mixture of briskness and kindness, tempered with a gentle irony. The watercolor pictures are brilliant, offering a privileged view into a fully realized imaginary world. Even the volumes themselves, made small according to Potter's own instructions to fit into children's hands, seem to invite your child to take them up and enjoy them.

Potter's most famous story, *The Tale of Peter Rabbit,* began in 1893 as a letter with accompanying pictures on the page to cheer up the sick child of her friend and former governess, Annie Carter Moore. In 1901, at thirty-five, Potter, on the advice of another friend, decided to expand this story about

Peter Rabbit and submit it for publication. The first publisher who saw it, Frederick Warne and Company, sent it back, as did the next half-dozen publishers.

Undaunted, Potter was determined to publish *Peter Rabbit* on her own, and for eleven pounds she had 250 copies printed, with black-and-white illustrations and a color frontispiece showing Peter being dosed with camomile tea by his mother. She sold them to friends and relatives—Sir Arthur Conan Doyle, creator of Sherlock Holmes, bought one for his children—and cleared a modest profit. By the time she was ready to order another 200 copies from the printer, Frederick Warne offered to publish *Peter Rabbit,* on the condition that Potter provide color illustrations throughout the story, and so began a magic kingdom that your own child can now visit and appreciate.

OPEN one of the tales with your child, and together you'll find a fantasy world that seems distant yet very near, as if you might be able to catch sight of Peter Rabbit himself through the nursery window, if only you awakened early enough. Part of the magic lies in Potter's meticulously exact detail in her renderings of flowers and plants—they are, in fact, entirely realistic and drawn precisely to scale—and the way those images blend with her animal-human characters to make us believe in them, too. And there are the homes of those characters, also rendered with fully realistic detail—the tidy house under the hedge, where Mrs. Tittlemouse polishes her tin spoons; Mrs. Tiggy-winkle's farmhouse, with its flagged floors and wooden beams; and Mrs. Rabbit's kitchen, complete with vegetables and saucepans. It's a world at once familiar and fantastic, its tiny scale and clarity especially suited to a child's view.

While the pictures are inviting to young eyes, they are never patronizing. Instead, Potter strives to make the complex simple and the simple beautiful. When you read *Peter Rabbit* to your child, notice the composition of the pictures, especially the way Peter's presence is always felt, even when the only sign of him is the tips of his ears or his lost shoe.

Take a close look at the illustration that shows Peter by the wheelbarrow. A typical Potter watercolor, it's a perfect companion to the words on the opposite page, capturing exactly the lushness of the garden and the danger of the moment. At this point, you're reading a description of Peter as he tries to find some way out of Mr. McGregor's garden. Desperate and frightened, he hears the "scratch, scritch" of Mr. McGregor hoeing onions and then sees the gate beyond him. Should Peter make a run for it?

The picture shows us his dilemma simply and graphically. In a line from foreground to background, we see Peter himself, surrounded by tender green plants, Mr. McGregor with his back turned, and the small white gate not too far in the distance. It's quite a riveting illustration, for its beauty as well as its importance to the story. Clearly, it's a place to pause, to let your child see the story you've been reading dramatized in a single, memorable image.

I had no idea just how much Potter had told her story of Peter Rabbit through the pictures, in fact, until my three-year-old daughter surprised me with a comment at the conclusion of the book. As I read of Mrs. Rabbit preparing to dose her disobedient son with the dreadful camomile tea, Franny sighed thoughtfully. "She should have known."

Amused, I asked her how Mrs. Rabbit could have predicted that Peter would go into Mr. McGregor's garden rather than down the lane to pick blackberries with the other bunnies.

Franny took the book from my hands, turning back through the pages until she came to the illustration of Mrs. Rabbit handing the berry baskets to her children.

"See?" she pointed out to me with authority.

I looked, and saw for the first time how Flopsy, Mopsy, and Cottontail were gathered around their mother, almost clamoring for the baskets, while Peter stood apart, his back turned, his hands deep in his pockets.

"He's not going berry picking."

Of course not! He's the very picture of determined disobedience, an image that usually escapes adult attention, but draws a child into its meaning readily.

Beatrix Potter had faith in the keen eyes of her "readers" when she composed these exquisite illustrations and filled them with telling as well as graceful details. The eyes of a young child see with an unsurpassed acuity, as every illustrator of children's books knows, and the colorful pictures that delight children can also bring them closer to the mystery in black-and-white on the opposite pages.

LIKE the watercolors of Beatrix Potter, the pen-and-ink drawings by E. H. Shepard for A. A. Milne's *Winnie-the-Pooh* and *The House at Pooh Corner* capture those moments most interesting to young children—eating, playing, and what Eeyore dolefully refers to as "the social round." As one of the primary architects of the world of the magic kingdom, Shepard helps your child to imagine childhood as an actual landscape of his own, with trees to climb and journeys to go on, just as in the map of the Hundred Acre Wood that opens the story.

And here, at the center of this world of childhood, is Christopher Robin—standing in command over his "expotition," gazing with gentle concern upon his poor, confused Pooh Bear, rescuing him from all kinds of real and imagined dangers. For it is Shepard's illustrations of Christopher Robin at play in the Forest that first welcome your child inside, invite her to put herself in the character's place, to rule with natural benevolence and wisdom.

As Shepard's pictures make clear, Christopher Robin is the ruler of this magic kingdom, and it is the visual renderings we get of his reactions that tell us what's happening in the story. Has Piglet really encountered a Fierce Heffalump, as he tells Christopher Robin? No, because on the same page we see Christopher Robin jumping up and down and laughing at what he hears. How serious is Tigger's bouncing that lands

Eeyore in the river? Not very, we know, since we see Christopher Robin playing Poohsticks with his friends on the bridge. Nothing can be all that terrible, your child understands, because Christopher Robin himself presides over this imaginary world with a calm and reassuring benevolence.

Fierce Heffalumps can be laughed away, and bouncings forgotten in games, but there is one problem—that of learning to read—that springs up again and again in the Forest, and must be faced and solved. It's a challenge that concerns not only Christopher Robin and Pooh, but your own child as well, and it's accorded special attention in Shepard's illustrations.

In fact, it's the subject of the first illustration opposite the author's Introduction, where we see Pooh staring down in bewilderment at a rectangular cloth with some reversed letters in the middle. He's scratching his head, trying to read the message, but he's obviously perplexed.

By the end of the first chapter, the mystery is solved. In the illustration at the bottom of the page, we see the cloth set right side up and placed where it should be. The letters BATH MAT are now clearly visible, next to the bath itself, and Pooh perches on the side of the tub, his nose high, a signal to us that he's pleased with himself.

Many of Shepard's most memorable illustrations include writing, not just as captions, but as an essential element of the picture. Making some kind of sense of the letters that appear again and again is an important part of the enjoyment of the story for your child. And in a real sense, it *is* the story, since the underlying direction of the *Pooh* books is the course from the nursery to the schoolroom, where Christopher Robin learns to read and write.

IN this magic kingdom, Christopher Robin's heroism arises out of his unfailing instinct for solving a problem definitively, with a minimum of embarrassment and without hurt feelings. It's a rare quality, one deeply appreciated by young children, who so often find themselves stuck in uncomfortable situations, in need of some quick thinking and a little understanding.

And "stuck" is exactly what Winnie-the-Pooh is, in one of the first and most memorable of his adventures. When he eats too much honey and condensed milk at Rabbit's house, Pooh becomes so full that he can't squeeze himself out the front door. Helplessly trapped, half-in and half-out, he looks to Christopher Robin for advice. His friend gently calms him, explaining that only time can get him out of this fix. If Pooh waits a week without eating, Christopher Robin tells him, then he'll become thin enough to be pulled through. In the meantime, Christopher Robin promises to read to him.

An illustration shows us Christopher Robin reading his alphabet book, open to "J for Jam," while Pooh listens with interest. Christopher Robin's earnestness, reflected in the way he cradles the book he's reading, and Pooh's fascination, which seems to overcome for the moment even the indignity of Rabbit's using his legs for a towel-horse, combine to create an image of the act of reading as a love feast.

In this case, "feast" is what it is, since reading is the only food Pooh can enjoy for now. If he's to get out into the world, Pooh has to control his hunger for condensed milk and honey and concentrate instead on the imaginary jam Christopher Robin offers him through reading. And it works. After a week passes, Christopher Robin, Rabbit, and all of Rabbit's friends and relations are able to pull Pooh from the hole like a cork out of a bottle, and the bear walks happily on his way.

You read to your child for some of the same reasons that Christopher Robin reads to Pooh—to comfort him, to offer him interesting things to think about, and ultimately to help him to get out into the world. Imaginary places such as the Forest, where questions and problems can be worked out on an understandable scale, are child-sized worlds waiting to be entered and explored. The Forest is a small fictional world, even for children, but it leads to larger ones like the River

Bank, Neverland, Narnia and Middle-earth, where bigger challenges await. For now—as if in preparation for the journey ahead—the prevailing question in the Forest involves what reading and writing are all about.

LITERACY, we soon find, is a chancy thing in the Forest, just as it is in childhood. Fluency in reading and writing depends in large part on a child's interest, which normally varies, even from day to day. That's why you encourage, but never force, your child to read as soon as he shows that he'd like to try. And once he's started, you don't insist or expect that his progress will be steady or predictable, because learning to read and write is a mysterious and personal process. The *Pooh* books affirm this truth with sensitivity and humor.

Christopher Robin's friends, with the exception of Tigger and Roo, all have some reading ability and general capacity for writing. They also face some of the ups and downs every child experiences in early reading. Eeyore's first glimmer of interest in the letter "A," which Christopher Robin has formed just for him out of three sticks, is quashed when Rabbit makes pedantic and overly critical remarks. Left to himself, though, Eeyore writes a poem for Christopher Robin—a present for a thoughtful teacher.

Pooh himself is characteristically humble about his reading and writing, confessing that his spelling is "wobbly," so the letters wind up in the wrong places. Out of self-consciousness, he asks for Owl's help in writing a birthday greeting to Eeyore. Owl's spelling is no better than Pooh's, but because of his confidence Owl writes fluently, if not very accurately. Still, Owl's long message requires the interpretation of the writer—a familiar circumstance, if you're one of the many parents whose child is intent on writing himself into literacy.

Rabbit loves to write out orders and leave them about the Forest, coming around to his friends afterward to read them aloud with a great deal of self-importance. But when Christopher Robin leaves his own written message—GON OUT BACKSON BISY BACKSON C. R.—and Rabbit can't figure out what BACKSON means, he asks Owl for help. Although Owl has no more notion of what it means than Rabbit, he takes a stab at it—a good strategy for those learning to read—and guesses from the context that it's some kind of animal that must be going around with Christopher Robin these days. Rabbit, true to form, takes the opportunity to interrogate Pooh closely about this elusive "Backson," with no success. But time unravels the mystery, and by the end of the chapter, everything is clear. Christopher Robin was "bisy" learning to read and write, and his next note reflects this change: GONE OUT BACK SOON C. R.

The *Pooh* books reassure your child—and, not incidentally, remind you—that learning to read and to write isn't an automatic, mechanical process, but a complex and very personal challenge that involves a great deal of self-expression. That's why each of the Forest animals goes about it in his own way: Eeyore mulls it over alone, Rabbit uses it to dominate others, and Owl tries to appear wiser than he really is. And Pooh seems still to be overwhelmed by the prospect of literacy, despite his wonderful talent for composing "hums" by ear.

A GREAT part of the enjoyment in reading the *Pooh* books to your child lies in the way both of you are able to see and understand what the characters can't at first. For children who are learning to read, and even for those who are learning to be read to, the experience is empowering as well as fun.

When my daughter Franny was little more than four, we read the story of the rainstorm that traps Piglet high in his tree house. Panicked, he writes a note that he puts in a bottle and tosses out into the water, hoping someone will find it and rescue him. On one side, he writes simply "Help!" and signs his name, with the explanation "(Me)." But on the other side of the note is the message "Its Me Piglit, Help Help."

When we came to the second message, Franny laughed with delight. "He thinks the paper can talk!" she explained to me, sensing here a subtle yet essential difference between spoken and written language. It's a distinction you wouldn't ordinarily think of explaining to a young child, important though it is. Fortunately, if you're reading *Pooh* together, the point will be made simply and memorably, with laughter.

IN the magic kingdom of the Forest, Christopher Robin meets the challenges of reading and writing in a way his friends never will. He is the ruler of this magic kingdom, and everything and everyone within its boundaries exist so that he will grow within it, and, ultimately, beyond it. In the meantime, Pooh Bear and the rest make all the mistakes so that Christopher Robin—and your child, too—can learn from them.

When "Pooh and Piglet Go Hunting and Nearly Catch a Woozle," for example, the two friends work themselves up into (literally) a fever pitch over the strange pawprints they track around a group of trees. Is it a Woozle? A Wizzle? Whatever it is, it seems to be gathering others like it at an alarming rate, Pooh and Piglet judge from the increasing numbers of separate pawprints before them as they circle around and around.

Your child giggles in anticipation during this tale, because it's so abundantly clear from the description and illustrations that Pooh and Piglet are tracking their own pawprints around the tree. Their attempts to appear unruffled despite their mounting anxiety are familiar tricks to the youngest listeners. When Pooh suddenly stops and points excitedly, crying, "*Look!*" Piglet jumps in alarm—"*What?*"—and then, to hide his fright, casually jumps "up and down once or twice in an exercising sort of way."

There's no Woozle, or Wizzle, of course, although Piglet runs off in terror before he knows this. It's Pooh who makes the discovery, because he stays to hear the viewpoint of Christopher Robin, who has been sitting in the tree all the while, watching his good friends circling around and around beneath him. Suddenly startled into seeing the truth of the situation when he places his paw in one of the prints and finds that it fits exactly, Pooh's embarrassed. "I have been Foolish and Deluded," he says, "and I am a Bear of No Brain at All." But this isn't the proper lesson for Winnie-the-Pooh, and his young friend soothes him with loving assurance, "You're the Best Bear in All the World." And Pooh trots off happily to lunch.

Christopher Robin's stature here is literal as well as figurative. High in the tree, he sees—just as your child sees—what Pooh and Piglet can't, and his perspective is clearly the better one for figuring out the situation. But Christopher Robin doesn't use his advantage to belittle Pooh. On the contrary, he praises his Bear, and the conclusion returns everything in the Forest to its usual happy state.

EVEN repeated mistakes cause no lasting problems or damage, as we see when "Piglet Meets a Heffalump." In conversation with Pooh and Piglet, Christopher Robin happens to mention that he recently saw a "Heffalump"—his pronunciation of "elephant"—at the zoo. Later that day, fired by a sudden desire for adventure, Pooh and Piglet determine to trap a Heffalump, without knowing exactly what it is. Just as they carefully tracked the Woozle around the tree, Pooh and Piglet earnestly plan to bait and capture a Heffalump, but end up, as before, only frightening themselves.

Pooh and Piglet's ideas are always only partly ridiculous. Their methods follow logically—one does, after all, trace pawprints to find an animal and use bait to trap it—but like most children, Pooh and Piglet just don't know enough about the world to understand fully what's happening. The fun of the stories comes from your own child's ability to see further than Pooh and Piglet can, and so anticipate what will come as a surprise to them. Only when the young listener is thoroughly confident about what's really going on does Christopher Robin himself appear, representing your child, to explain the situation to his friends, and to correct it.

Piglet digs a hole for the Heffalump trap and Pooh gets a jar of honey for bait, reasoning that since honey would tempt him, it would doubtless tempt a Heffalump. The two friends part and agree to meet early the next morning to see not *if,* but *how many* Heffalumps they've caught.

That night, disturbed by visions of Heffalumps devouring all his honey, Pooh decides to retrieve the bait and eat it himself. Returning to the trap, he goes so far as to push his head entirely inside the honey pot, eager to get the last lick at the bottom of the jar. Meanwhile, Piglet, dreading the possibility of actually coming face-to-face with a Very Fierce Animal, has come early to the trap as well, in order to take a peek and quietly flee if a Heffalump is there. Just as Piglet approaches the trap, Pooh realizes that he can't get the honey pot off his head and roars in misery. "And it was at that moment," we learn, "that Piglet looked down."

Everything is hilariously clear to your child, of course. Otherwise, Piglet's hysterical cries wouldn't be funny at all. Christopher Robin himself, when brought back to the trap by the quivering Piglet, cannot help laughing at the sight of the "herrible hoffalump" that his friend has described as looking like "an enormous big nothing. Like a jar." In fact, it's laughter that seems to solve the problem and reveal the reality of the situation. It's not until Christopher Robin laughs that Pooh manages to crack the jar against a tree root and free his head. Laughing is just the thing to do, it seems. And your child laughs first.

EVERYONE in the *Pooh* books struggles with more or less success to decipher and to use letters, so the writing in the pictures is really an invitation to your child to join the action, too. In chapter after chapter, Christopher Robin and his friends experiment with reading and writing—jotting down notes, making lists, lettering signs, deciphering messages, all with enthusiasm and with varying degrees of accuracy. You'll enjoy letting your child in on the joke about Piglet's mistaken interpretation of the broken sign TRESPASSERS W outside his house (he firmly believes that it's short for "Trespassers William," his grandfather). And your child will be pleased when she can sound out for herself the label on Pooh's treasured jars—HUNNY.

But just when you might begin to believe that Shepard has prepared all his illustrations to favor the literate, there's a triumph for sharp-eyed prereaders. Eeyore, it seems, has lost his tail, a misfortune Shepard presents in four small pictures of the donkey turning this way and that in an effort to get a look for himself. Pooh, determined to find the tail for his friend, goes to Owl's house for advice, and is met at the door by two signs written by Christopher Robin.

The illustration shows Pooh puzzling over these messages, which instruct the visitor to PLES RING IF AN RNSER IS REQIRD and PLEZ CNOKE IF AN RNSR IS NOT REQID. Unsure, Pooh rings, knocks, and then, for good measure, calls out to Owl for help, but after a long, unsatisfying conversation is no closer to recovering Eeyore's tail—or so he thinks.

It's when Owl escorts Pooh out again to show him the new bell-pull he's just found in a bush that the light dawns. In Shepard's larger, close-up view of Owl's front door, above one of the baffling signs, the bell-pull is revealed as Eeyore's lost tail—a discovery, thanks to Shepard, that Pooh and your child make at precisely the same moment.

Pooh retrieves it, of course, and the next picture shows Christopher Robin carefully nailing it back where it belongs. Shepard then includes four more illustrations of Eeyore, this time in an uncharacteristically joyful mood, frisking about in triumph over his recovered tail. The point of real reading, we see, is not just deciphering letters, but seeing and understanding what is important. And the importance of learning to make such connections is the continuing story of the *Pooh* books, a lesson taught through and celebrated in Shepard's pictures.

At the end of *Winnie-the-Pooh,* Christopher Robin presents his Bear with a special pencil case, just like his, so Pooh can write messages, too. In fact, we can see it tucked carefully under his arm in the last illustration as he walks off with Piglet. But in the final chapter of *The House at Pooh Corner,* we come to realize that Christopher Robin must go on to make connections and work with symbols in a way Pooh never can. Literacy lies beyond the magic kingdom of the Forest, but the road to it is straight through its heart, in the illustrations. Once your child learns to find meaning on a page by calling on imagination and memory, she's well on her way to being a real reader. And, like Christopher Robin himself, you can both say, "Mr Shepard Helpd."

WE leave childhood and then discover it all over again with our children. Perhaps the most precise expression of this truth is Shepard's last illustration in the *Pooh* books, when we leave Christopher Robin and Pooh in the Enchanted Place at the top of the wood, where, despite the realities of time and growth, the narrator promises us "a little Boy and his Bear will always be playing."

It's an uncharacteristic picture for Shepard. Christopher Robin and Pooh are presented as never before, simply as black silhouettes against a minimal landscape, just enough to show them romping off happily together. They seem almost to have gone from the page entirely, leaving behind their shapes, like footprints, as proof that they were once there. It's a picture that combines absence and presence quite memorably, and sums up for us in a single image what every parent—and, perhaps, every child—knows about the mystery and beauty of childhood, lost and found.

CHAPTER THREE

Outside Over There

YOU bring home a new book for your young child and she opens it eagerly, turning the pages and looking intently at the pictures. Even before you read the story, she's already on the road to the magic kingdom, finding the way with her acute child-sight. You may wonder, as you watch her happily poring over the illustrations to extract their meaning, whether what she's up to is itself a form of reading—a purely visual capacity that is not so much the inability to read words as the ability to do without them.

But soon she will come to you and place the book in your hands, so she can hear as well as see the story unfold. And as she sits on your lap and listens, still looking at the pictures, the gates of the magic kingdom swing open, unlocked by the combination of her visual and imaginative gifts and your voice. For parent and child, the best way to say "open sesame" is "Let's read together."

After you've read the new book to her once, twice, several times, you'll notice a change in the way she looks through it. She concentrates just as intently upon the illustrations, but now she's talking while she looks. What she says may not match exactly the words in the book, but the point is, having experienced the pleasure that comes from combining sight and sound when you read together, she's determined to do it on her own.

After you read the book several more times with her, she'll return to it by herself, and you may hear distinct words and phrases from the story emerging, usually prompted by an appropriate picture. And don't be surprised to find that your child is soon turning the pages at precisely the correct time, because, with your help, she's now discovered how to open the gates of the magic kingdom all by herself.

* * *

MAURICE Sendak's stories are usually among the first books to be taken up by young children today. Once drawn into Sendak's wildly enchanted world by his pictures, illustrations as evocative and fascinating as anything by Tenniel or Shepard, your child will find the language of the book irresistible—by turns funny, haunting, and lyrical, often rhyming and always memorable. Even to adults, Sendak's words seem to carry the power of an incantation. When spoken aloud and placed next to his illustrations, they give the exciting illusion of calling that picture-world into life. No wonder, then, that your child memorizes Sendak's stories so quickly, because to be able to speak the words aloud is to be part of the magic.

Just as in other earlier classic stories, Sendak's child characters enter another world, triumph in it, and then return home having learned an important lesson about growing up. The energetic Max of *Where the Wild Things Are* is sent to bed without supper because he has answered his mother's orders to calm down with the shout "I'll eat you up!" But his confinement turns into an adventure when a forest grows magically inside his room, an ocean appears, and he sails in a boat to where the wild things are.

Max, of course, is a wild thing himself—we have his mother's word for it—so when the creatures he meets do their worst to scare him, he tames them by staring at them (the magic power of child-sight!), proving himself "the wildest thing of all." The other wild things proclaim him king—yet another child's coronation in the magic kingdom—and after a royal romp among them, Max tries on his mother's role and sends them all to bed without supper. While they sleep, Max becomes lonely and prepares to leave for that other world, "where someone loved him best of all." The wild things demand that he stay ("We'll eat you up, we love you so!"), but Max leaves in the same magical way he came and returns to his room.

The land of "where the wild things are," like other magic kingdoms of childhood imagination, is a place both far and near, found only by those it chooses. For Max, it is the place where a game of wildness and control can heal the breach that has temporarily come between him and his mother. In the world of the wild things, Max tries life from his mother's perspective while keeping his own wild essence, and he hears his wild subjects express both love and anger simultaneously ("We'll eat you up, we love you so!"), which puts him at ease about his own impulsive yelling as well as his mother's response to it. And sure enough, when Max returns to his room, he finds that anger doesn't cancel out love in this world either. His supper is waiting for him, and it's still hot.

SENDAK's Ida of *Outside Over There* is, like Max, a child who insists on independence, but she's a few years older, and she needs to be assured of her own ability rather than her parents' love. *Outside Over There* presents a more complex story, a game played for higher stakes than *Where the Wild Things Are,* but Ida, we see, learns something important about the everyday world by entering another world, just as Max does.

While her sailor father is at sea and her mother is in the arbor, Ida is given the responsibility of watching the baby. She plays her "wonder horn" to soothe her sister, but will not look at her. In picture after picture, we see Ida's eyes averted, her gaze somewhere else. This single bit of willfulness is enough to open a passage for evil to enter: unobserved, goblins push through a window and kidnap the baby, leaving behind an ice-doll.

Ida realizes the switch when she embraces the substitute, and immediately springs into action. Wrapping herself in her mother's raincloak and taking along her horn, she sets forth to rescue her sister, but repeats her mistake by climbing, without looking, "backwards out her window into outside over there."

Her carelessness causes her to lose the way to the goblins' hidden world, but at last she hears her father's voice from over the sea, encouraging her to turn around again and to use the power of her music to rescue the baby. Ida follows her

[49]

father's advice, finds the way, saves her sister, and returns home with her safely.

Your child will enjoy delightful shivers in seeing the goblins silently stalking while Ida looks away, unaware of the danger. The penetration of one world by another is eerie and malevolent—not at all like the forest that suddenly grows in Max's room—but its might is matched and at last undone by the power of love. The goblins may "push their way in" at Ida's window, but Ida's father can reach her when she's lost between worlds, and his song helps her to find both the way to her sister and the means to free her.

And the father's message is a suggestion rather than a command, a gentle reminder from a loving parent to a child to use *all* her strengths, not just one. Ida's acuity for hearing and listening is clear, and has made her a musician, but she needs to use her eyes, to *look* as well as to hear, or she'll be lost. It is only when Ida learns from her mistake, and puts sight and sound together, that she can enter the goblin world and rescue her sister.

When she arrives home, Ida finds a more conventional message from her father—a letter—that reminds her again to watch the baby, which, we are assured, is "just what Ida did." Now the illustrations show Ida looking attentively at her toddling sister and, significantly, gazing over her mother's shoulder at the letter itself.

Is Ida reading now? It may be, since she's found the connection between seeing and hearing and proved its power to herself. And, by happy coincidence, you're accomplishing the same purpose by reading Ida's story with your own child on your lap, the book open before you both. In reading together, you'll show your child the power of sight and sound, and invite her to find for herself the connection between them, so she can explore new worlds "outside over there," and beyond.

SENDAK'S stories can point the way to the magic kingdom of imagination for your child at a very early age. As soon as he understands his first story, your child gets a glimpse of the land just beyond our sight where a child hero rules, faces challenges, and triumphs.

Your child is naturally curious about anything that's just over the horizon. It is the compulsion to satisfy this curiosity that is the essence of childhood. So you don't have to explain to your child why, for instance, Peter Rabbit goes to Mr. McGregor's garden, despite the danger. He goes for the same reason Alice follows the White Rabbit, or the four children of the Narnia tales enter the wardrobe. It's the same instinct that compels your own growing child; the overwhelming need to see and to understand for himself what he doesn't yet know.

Reading your child stories about characters who feel the same desire as he does to explore and to understand is a way of creating and nurturing an imaginative connection with books. It's the vital link, as important in its way as the connection between sight and sound, and an essential part of learning to read. It's also an essential part of the growth of identity, because in characters such as Alice, Christopher Robin, Peter, Susan, Edmund, and Lucy, your child finds another self—someone just like him in some ways, but very different in others. By traveling along with these characters, seeing with their eyes, your child explores their possibilities and perspectives, and tries out new and different ways of looking at the world.

You'll know that your child has made this imaginative connection with books when you see him become so absorbed in a story that he plays at being the main character. And if you watch him from a distance, without him knowing that you're there, you'll be astonished to see how complete his identification with the character is. It's not so much pretending to be as it is virtually *becoming* a character in active play, spontaneously, and purely for the joy of the experience itself. Here, as you watch, your child is experimenting with identity, trying on a role, and ultimately creating a self.

The connections between books, play, and identity help children to grow through imagination. The play that makes a story a personal adventure for your child opens up new possibilities that broaden his perspectives. The ability to see and to understand more inspires him to search for another story, with a farther horizon. Once that horizon is met, another appears, so that childhood is a continual journey of discovery into outside over there, from magic kingdom to magic kingdom.

CLASSIC books inspire creative play. And sometimes a child's creative play can inspire a classic book, like *Winnie-the-Pooh,* first published in 1926. Before Winnie-the-Pooh was a character, he was the favorite toy and constant companion of a little boy whose formal name was Christopher Robin Milne, but who was known in the family as "Moon," after a very early attempt to pronounce his last name. Moon had his bear since he was a year old, but the name "Winnie-the-Pooh" came later, in honor of a swan called "Pooh," and a Canadian bear—"Winnie," short for Winnipeg—who was much loved by Moon and the other children who visited the London Zoo.

Because Moon was an only child, his growing imagination and social instincts found an outlet with his toys: Pooh, the oldest and best-loved; Piglet, smaller and newer; and Eeyore, a donkey whose neck could no longer support his drooping head, and so always looked melancholy. On the floor of the nursery they played—Moon speaking and responding for them—a little community of friends who understood one another.

His mother, Daphne, would join in occasionally, also talking for the toys and thinking up new situations and ideas for them, while Moon's father, Alan, looked on. He wasn't the sort of parent who gets down on the floor with his child, but he did enter the play in his own way. He watched as Moon's love gave life to his toys, as Daphne's interest broadened their horizons, and then he went to his writing desk.

* * *

ALAN Alexander Milne described himself as the kind of man who succeeded because he was "not wholly the wrong person, in the right spot at the right moment." He was an indifferent student at Cambridge University, despite early promise as a mathematician. Shortly after he turned to writing light verse, he became the editor of *Granta,* the Cambridge literary journal. From there he walked easily into the offices of *Punch,* where he found himself assistant editor at the age of twenty-four.

After Milne spent a few years turning out weekly material for *Punch,* the First World War intervened. When Milne returned to London, he discovered that the most immediate effect of the war, for him at least, was that he had lost his position, and consequently would never be editor-in-chief of *Punch,* as he had planned. He tried the theatre instead, and, with the encouragement of his friend J. M. Barrie, author of *Peter Pan,* wrote and produced several plays. One of them— *Mr. Pim Passes By*—was so enthusiastically received that people began comparing Milne to George Bernard Shaw. It was another early sign of promise that was not to come to full fruition.

Success began to elude him at the office and in the theatre, but, with typical Milne luck, it turned out to be waiting for him in the nursery. As a kind of valentine, Milne presented his wife, Daphne, with "Vespers," a poem inspired by three-year-old Moon.

> Little Boy kneels at the foot of the bed,
> Droops on the little hands little gold head.
> Hush! Hush! Whisper who dares!
> Christopher Robin is saying his prayers.

Milne was surprised by the ease with which he could write the verses. "Christopher Robin" was the perfect name for the rhythm of such poetry, he soon found.

When Daphne sent the poem to *Vanity Fair* and immediately received a check in return, Milne determined to write more children's poems. His first collection, *When We Were Very Young,* was published in 1924 and quickly sold half a million copies. It included a poem, "Halfway Down," that seems to reveal Milne's first imaginings of a magic kingdom, a place both far and near where anything can happen. The step "halfway down" the stairs, a child tells us, is his favorite place to stop, because it doesn't seem to have any defined location at all. Like any good magic kingdom, it exists only in childhood imagination:

> It isn't really
> Anywhere!
> It's somewhere else
> Instead!

At the beginning of *Winnie-the-Pooh,* Christopher Robin himself comes down the stairs with Pooh bumping after him and asks, on Pooh's behalf, for a story about his bear. The chapters that follow are a father's generous answer to that request. As you read the book to your child, you take on the voice of the author, dramatizing and elaborating the adventures of a child's imaginary friends, creating a world where Pooh and the others struggle with the daily problems of childhood. And your child becomes Christopher Robin, the king and guardian of this realm, and the person who gives this world its purpose.

The magic kingdom of *Winnie-the-Pooh*—the Forest— seems like a glorious backyard just on the other side of Christopher Robin's green door. And, in fact, the inspiration for it was the land surrounding the family's country house, Cotchford Farm, in Sussex, where Moon enjoyed the freedom he couldn't in London. Wherever he went he took Pooh, and Moon's Nanny accompanied them both as they wandered happily, splashing across streams, balancing on branches, making a little house in a hollow walnut tree.

The countryside was full of exciting places to discover, like the six pine trees and the great expanse of ancient beech trees called the Five Hundred Acre Wood. Just inside this wood

Moon found an astounding tree with a long branch extending outward and then sloping gently to the forest floor, almost as if it were a stairway to a house. Moon was so taken with this particular tree that he brought his parents to see him walk along the branch toward the trunk, as if to knock on the door of whoever might live inside (Owl, as it turns out). Later, when E. H. Shepard came to Cotchford, he made this curious tree the subject of two of his illustrations for *Winnie-the-Pooh,* and re-created the memorable stroll along the branch with Pooh in Moon's place.

Moon's play inspired his father's books, and when you read *Winnie-the-Pooh* and *The House at Pooh Corner* to your own child, the books will, in turn, inspire *his* play. In fantasy, your child will become the Christopher Robin who rules the magic kingdom of the Forest, and Pooh will become his companion, too. Your child identifies with "Good King Christopher," who loves his subjects despite their frailty and occasional silliness. From Christopher Robin's privileged perspective, your child can see Pooh, Piglet, Eeyore, Rabbit, and the rest of the Forest's inhabitants come to terms with the special problems of growing up and living together. Greediness, fear, jealousy—all are faced and happily overcome with the help of Christopher Robin, who is himself learning and growing.

IN Christopher Robin's magic kingdom, where the animals stand in for younger versions of himself (and your child), growing up is sometimes difficult, and involves making mistakes and learning from them. Most of all, it involves change and the acceptance of change.

Throughout the story, Christopher Robin shows himself willing to adjust, but some of his Forest friends—Rabbit in particular—fight against changes, like the arrival of Kanga and Roo, or the unique "bounciness" of the new Tigger. Occasionally, change is stubbornly opposed, and then we see the uncomfortable—but funny—results.

When the mother Kanga and baby Roo suddenly appear in

the Forest, Pooh is bewildered, but accepts Christopher Robin's casual explanation that they arrived "in the Usual Way." Still puzzled, Pooh joins Piglet and Rabbit to talk the whole thing over. All are uneasy about the change in their world, much as an older child feels some resentment and jealousy when faced with the prospect of sharing his home with a newborn brother or sister.

Left to themselves, Pooh and Piglet would probably have gotten over their worry eventually and enjoyed having new friends, but Rabbit suddenly determines to drive Kanga and Roo out of the Forest and restore what he sees as the natural order. Part of Rabbit's plan involves switching Piglet and Roo, and holding the baby until the mother agrees to leave. But when Kanga discovers Piglet in her pouch instead of Roo, she doesn't panic or plead for her baby, as Rabbit expected. Instead, she simply treats Piglet as if he were Roo, washing, feeding, and gently scolding him. Although Piglet indignantly protests all this baby pampering, Kanga ignores him.

Every big brother or sister wishes at some point to change places with the baby, to be fussed over and pampered. In Piglet's experience, we get a glimpse of what it would be like to be given a baby's attention after the need for it has been outgrown. The reality, it's clear, is much more like a comic nightmare than a dream come true. Better, certainly, to be grown up and accept the new situation rather than to resent the baby and plot to take his place.

The House at Pooh Corner offers another look at the problem of sibling jealousy. This time the focus is Tigger, who finds a home at Kanga's as a sort of big brother to Roo. Both Kanga and Roo are delighted with Tigger's lively company, but the rest of the Forest community—again, Rabbit in particular—objects to Tigger's "bounciness."

Rabbit's misguided plan for "unbouncing" the large, energetic Tigger calls for losing him in the Forest in order to teach him a lesson. When they find Tigger again, Rabbit promises Pooh and Piglet, he'll be easier to live with, "Because he'll be a Humble Tigger. Because he'll be a Sad Tigger, a Melancholy Tigger, a Small and Sorry Tigger, and

Oh-Rabbit-I-*am*-glad-to-see-you Tigger." It's a more serious, thought-out plan than the Piglet–Roo switch, and re-
sembles the work of an older child expressing annoyance
with a younger sibling's hijinks.

The second plan actually works very well. The one who is
lost in the Forest does come back sad and demoralized, having learned a lesson—but it's Rabbit and not Tigger. Tigger,
we learn later, will never stop bouncing. Like Kanga and
Roo, the change he brings must simply be accepted. Fighting
against change leads only to the loss of one's self, as both
Piglet and Rabbit find, in their own ways.

THE *Pooh* books always emphasize the advantage of knowing
over not knowing, being older rather than younger, and being able to accept change instead of fighting it. And the conclusion of *The House at Pooh Corner* offers the life lesson for
which all the stories have been preparing us. Ultimately,
Christopher Robin must leave the Forest to go to school,
because he is growing up. Our experience tells us this is
good: learning is more comfortable than confusion, growing
up brings independence, and change should be welcomed.

Christopher Robin accepts the impending change in his
life. Although he is disappointed by the loss of his freedom to
"do nothing" whenever he wants, he is still pleased by the
prospect of a new outside over there, beyond the Forest,
where he can learn about such exotic things as Factors and
Knights and what comes from Brazil. He even bridges the
gap between his life in the Forest and his school life by knight-
ing Pooh, a rite that unites the old and new knowledge while
honoring Pooh's special place in his life. It is an act in which
Good King Christopher at once immortalizes his magic kingdom and leaves it for a farther horizon.

Earlier, in *Winnie-the-Pooh*, Christopher Robin celebrates
his bear's unique gifts and acknowledges his reliance on Pooh
to save the day. Christopher Robin energetically assembles
all his friends on what Pooh calls an "expotition" to the
North Pole, and enacts in play the journey of discovery un-

dertaken by every child in growing up. He leads his friends bravely and wisely toward their goal, but then, after a halt for lunch, Christopher Robin draws Rabbit aside and admits that he's not entirely sure what a North Pole looks like, or how to find it. Such uncertainty—about the unknown, about the future itself—is a normal part of every child's life, and even Christopher Robin can't avoid it entirely.

While they puzzle over this mystery of the North Pole, baby Roo suddenly falls in the stream. Kanga shouts and runs alongside Roo as he's carried farther and farther downstream by the current. Owl stays where he is and quotes some very sensible advice, Piglet jumps up and down, squealing in anxiety, and Eeyore offers assistance by putting his tail in the water, though much too far away to be of any help to Roo.

By the time Rabbit has recovered himself sufficiently to shout for someone to get something across the stream for Roo to catch on to, Pooh is already there, holding a pole across the stream. On the other bank, Kanga takes an end, and Roo is rescued.

Pooh can't explain how he thought of what to do or where he found the pole. But he's saved Roo and, as Christopher Robin tells him, he's fulfilled the goal of the "expotition." Pooh's pole, Christopher Robin declares, is none other than the North Pole, a fact that the expedition formally acknowledges with a sign reading:

NorTH POLE

DICSovERED By PooH

PooH FouND IT

When Christopher Robin can't make the connections he needs to reach his goal, it's Winnie-the-Pooh's imagination that saves the day. To have Pooh Bear for your friend, then, is to draw on a kind of understanding that may not be able to explain itself, but can link ideas with facts, symbols with reality, and people with people in a way that explains everything else.

Even the ruler of a magic kingdom, it seems, needs the help of "the Best Bear in all the World." The friendship of Christopher Robin and Pooh shows your child the link between new and old knowledge, between the head and the heart, in children and in all of us. No one ever outgrows the need for imaginative understanding, and that's why Christopher Robin and Pooh can never really be parted, why "in that enchanted place on the top of the Forest, a little boy and his Bear will always be playing."

THE Forest of *Winnie-the-Pooh* and *The House at Pooh Corner* is an enchanted place, where the only danger lies in misunderstanding. Everything that seems confusing—friendship, growth, a few words on a piece of paper—turns out to be quite simple, if only you've got the right perspective. And even the most critical connection can be made easily, with a pole that's close to hand.

The stream that runs through this magic kingdom moves like a child, Milne explains, "quickly, eagerly, having so much to find out before it was too late." It slows down only at the very edge of the Forest, where it becomes "almost a river," and continues out of sight. It is at this point, from the bridge near the edge of the Forest, that Christopher Robin and his friends play Poohsticks, dropping twigs on one side of the bridge and then watching from the other side to see whose stick the current will carry through first. And in the magic kingdom of a child's imagination, a twig dropped from Poohsticks Bridge may very well float gently down this stream that is "almost a river" and suddenly be carried swiftly into that body of water whose name is simply and majestically "*the* River" of Kenneth Grahame's *The Wind in the Willows*.

Milne was not only delighted but clearly influenced by Grahame's classic story of Ratty and Mole, Toad and Bad-ger, published in 1908, almost twenty years before *Winnie-the-Pooh*. Enthusiastically he read *The Wind in the Willows* to his son Moon, and wrote a dramatization of it for children, emphasizing its comic adventures, and called his play *Toad of Toad Hall*. In fact, Milne loved *The Wind in the Willows* so much that he thought at times that it was *he* who had actually written the book, and simply recommended it to Grahame.

FOR Grahame himself, "the River" of his imagination could take him back to his own youth, when he punted on the river Cherwell. An enthusiastic public-school boy at St. Edward's, Oxford, where he excelled both in academics and sports, he longed to go on to university at Oxford—the prospect of three more years of punting on the Cherwell delighted him—but his family didn't see the use of a degree. Instead they insisted that he take the position of a clerk in the Bank of England, and there he thrived, rising professionally in a way that was gratifying, if not actually exciting. The work was congenial, the atmosphere casual, even by modern standards, and he soon found a companion for rowing on the Thames, so he could continue to indulge his taste for boating. In its way, the Bank of England was another Oxford or *Punch,* a center of power in the British Empire that encouraged indi-viduality as well as a sense of importance.

Grahame started writing stories, first about respectable businessmen who suddenly run away to a life in the coun-try—these were published under the title *Pagan Papers*—then about children coming to terms with themselves, their imag-inations, and the unaccountable adults who try to discipline their high spirits but never fully succeed. His two collections of these later stories, *The Golden Age* and *Dream Days,* were great popular successes, and Grahame was singled out for praise by critics for the natural and unsentimental way he presented children.

A recurring idea in his work was the dream of a "Golden

City," a "Good Place," where everything was wonderful and children could be completely independent and happy. His young characters believe that such a place must exist in reality somewhere, and at times they set out to find it themselves. One child tells the others that he imagines they can get to the Golden City by boat on a river with meadows on both sides, and that the current would gently bring them along right up to the steps of the palace.

It sounds like a remembered dream of punting on the Cherwell, and a distant vision of the city Grahame had wished to enter as a young man, Oxford. But the quest is sweeter than the fulfillment. Whenever the children imagine the Golden City itself, Grahame's dream collapses into a riotous and oddly unjoyous profusion of candy and toys. The best part is invariably the anticipation, the approach—in other words, the River itself.

In one of their adventures, the boy who is the narrator meets a grown-up artist who believes in the Golden City, too. The man talks about it comfortably, even enthusiastically, to the boy's astonished delight, and they part after promising to meet again someday in the place they both long to be. The boy walks off feeling that at least one adult understands him, confident now that finding the Golden City will be "an easy matter."

It wasn't an easy matter for Grahame, who for years after the success of *Dream Days* didn't write at all. Finally, with no fixed plans or hopes, Grahame wrote down some stories about a Toad he had been telling his son Alastair. Apparently, it was then that Grahame was inspired to combine his idea of the Golden City with the beauty and happiness he associated with "messing about in boats." From these elements he created the River Bank, the magic kingdom of *The Wind in the Willows*.

LIKE Milne, Grahame became a classic children's author on the strength of a single, unforgettable landscape with a small set of extraordinary characters. Milne's characters are stuffed toys come to life, and part of their appeal lies in the ease of imagining Moon's bear, the Bear on the page, and the bear your child has tucked under her arm as one and the same. But the characters of *The Wind in the Willows* are all living animals, with more fully developed and complex human characteristics. Their wildness and their independence take them out of the category of lovable toys like Pooh. The River Bank is a magic kingdom that's closer to nature than to the nursery, a wider world than Christopher Robin's Forest.

When, after the triumph of the *Pooh* books, E. H. Shepard had the opportunity to illustrate a new edition of Grahame's *The Wind in the Willows,* he visited the author, who was then over seventy, in order to get some ideas about the look of the characters and the lay of the land they inhabited. As Shepard tells the story, Grahame himself warmed to the subject, regretting that age and disability prevented him from accompanying the artist personally on a walk through the landscape that had inspired his story. After searching his memory, Grahame gave Shepard specific instructions on where to go and what to look for along the banks of the River, where Ratty and Mole boated, and over the hill that led to the Wild Wood.

Shepard found his way through the meadows that autumn afternoon and filled his notebook with sketches. When Grahame saw the results of the country walk, he was gratified, and, although he died before the new edition was published, he was able to look through Shepard's drawings of Mole, Ratty, Badger, Toad and the rest and say simply, "I'm glad you've made them real."

When you read *The Wind in the Willows* to your child, it's still Shepard's inspired sketches of the inhabitants of the woods and meadows that somehow make the story and its characters real. Before knowing why Toad is so silly, even before hearing the very first of his ridiculous exploits, your child can see Toad's character in the illustrations. Chin held high, arm outstretched to present his latest toy, the canary-yellow cart, Toad is the picture of the braggart, a conceited nouveau riche styled in just the right manner to make him thoroughly understandable and amusing to your child.

And the pastoral Eden that is Grahame's River Bank is itself mapped out by Shepard, just as the Forest is in *Winnie-the-Pooh,* with notations for Toad Hall, Badger's House, and all the other landmarks we come to know. In fact, a single glance at this map brings back memories of all the adventures you read about in *The Wind in the Willows* when you were a child. Suddenly, you're ready to tell all about these old friends you've recognized. Up to the left, you point out to your child, is Toad, lazing in his wicker chair on the lawn of Toad Hall and planning, no doubt, his next excursion on the road. At the very bottom stands the gruff but well-meaning Badger outside his house on the edge of the Wild Wood, letting the weasels and stoats know he's about. You could ask your child to find Ratty, in his boat on the River. And last, in the center, is Mole, who has just left his hole and, in defiance of the busybody rabbits, is boldly running in their private road and on to the River, where he'll meet—but here you stop. You're ready now to turn to the first page, where this very story has its beginning, where poor, overworked Mole is just about to scramble up and out into the spring air, to discover for the first time the glories and pleasures of the River Bank.

THE River Bank is a very social place, and its challenges extend from getting along with a new friend for a pleasant afternoon to understanding the fine points of proper behavior at a formal dinner party. Learning the rules of social behavior is a full-time job for Mole, who is a newcomer to the River Bank. Good-hearted, curious, and eager to get out into the world, Mole is an easy character for your child to feel close to right away. Like a child, he's impetuous, scrambling out of his hole when called by an irresistible voice from outside over there. We're with him as he discovers the River Bank and its ways, and we watch him grow from an uncertain observer of this world to an entirely accepted and loved participant in it.

Unlike Grahame's earlier visions of a Golden City, with its vaguely unsatisfying cascades of playthings, the River Bank is not meant to be an escape from real life, but a way of coming to terms with it. As a magic kingdom, it's a place with a purpose, because the challenges offered here answer Mole's need to be active, to grow, and to be responsible. Like your own child, Mole feels he must get out into the world, to see more and do more—to *grow up*—not just because it's inevitable, but because it's irresistible. Once Mole feels the overwhelming urge to scramble "up, up, up" out of his hole and into the sun, the River Bank is there for him, not an elusive dream, but a living reality, the finding of it "an easy matter" after all.

Christopher Robin knows his Forest as well as he knows himself, and so he always acts with confidence, whether resolving disagreements, explaining, comforting, or making suggestions. But Mole is entering a new and unfamiliar world, and he has much to learn before he, like Alice in Wonderland, can trust his own good sense. Mole's challenge is to discover a relationship between himself and the world outside that will balance getting his own way with getting along. And what better place to learn balance than on the River, in a boat?

When Mole first comes scurrying from his hole, he's challenged by some busybody rabbits who demand that he pay a toll before he passes. Full of spirit, Mole keeps running and jeers, "Onion-sauce!" at the group, leaving them astounded. Like a child full of himself, his enthusiasm is his power at this point, and it's proof against anything that stands in his way. Yet Mole's spirit is about to be tempered by something more powerful, a "sleek, sinuous, full-bodied animal"—the River itself.

Spellbound, Mole sits by the River, thrilled by its very sight and sound, when Rat appears from out of his burrow on the opposite bank. After polite greetings and a short pause,

Ratty asks Mole if he'd like to come over, and Mole, suddenly wary and suspicious that Rat is joking, replies peevishly, "Oh, it's all very well to *talk*." But then he sees Ratty bring around a small boat, step in, and scull over to him. With a friendly briskness, Ratty beckons him to step in and sit down, and before he knows it, the delighted Mole is in a real boat on a real river for the first time.

Ironically, after all his wild, urgent enthusiasm to see and experience the world, Mole has nearly missed his first chance for an adventure. His sudden self-consciousness makes him doubt Ratty's friendly intentions, and in consequence his answer sounds almost hostile. Fortunately, Ratty can easily prove to Mole that the invitation is genuine. Once Mole is seated in the boat opposite Ratty, drifting downriver, his fears and self-consciousness melt away, and he can enjoy himself and his new friend.

Mole's experience is a classic example of "first day" worry, something everyone—especially a child—knows all too well. The summer when Franny was nine, she signed up for a new day camp, and she looked forward to it with great excitement. But the first morning, as we were getting ready to leave for the bus, she suddenly wondered aloud, "What if I don't like camp, and camp doesn't like me?" I was surprised to hear her say this, since for weeks she'd been so eager to start, but I answered by asking her what *she'd* say to someone who was a bit worried about it. Her face brightened at once, and she said, "I'd tell them, 'you probably *will* like it. Give it a chance.' "

It's normal to worry a little about beginning something new, but part of growing up is learning to put aside your anxiety and to concentrate instead on the good possibilities ahead. Mole's story and its happy ending—the start of his friendship with Ratty—offers you and your child an opportunity to talk over the challenges of beginning a new life, the ways in which our feelings can color how we see the world, and the wonderful things that can happen—or not happen—depending on whether or not we let them.

* * *

THE moment when Mole and Ratty scull downriver for the first time in the small blue-and-white boat marks the beginning of Mole's education in what the world has to offer and what he has to give. With Ratty as his teacher and acting as a kind of parent, Mole learns first to enjoy and then to take a responsible part in life on the River Bank. Along the way, Ratty generously includes Mole in all the plans for fun, hinting at his duties, and encouraging him to try everything worth doing. And, of course, according to Ratty, nothing is "half so much worth doing as simply messing about in boats."

After a wonderful day on the River together, Mole thoroughly agrees with Ratty on this point. In fact, he's so excited about boating that he begs for a turn at the oars. Ratty wisely refuses, explaining that he needs some lessons first, because rowing isn't as easy as it looks. But Mole's spirits are high again, just as they were when he first came out of his hole, and in his impatience, he won't take no for an answer. Despite the fact that he can't swim and has never managed a boat, Mole grabs the oars from Ratty and starts rowing, almost immediately upsetting the boat and everything in it.

After Ratty fishes him out, collects all their belongings, and rights the boat again, Mole apologizes for his behavior, and asks his friend to forgive him for his ungratefulness. Mole despairs, not just because he's given himself a dunking, but because the whole day seems entirely ruined by a moment's thoughtlessness. He'd been so carefully polite all afternoon, asking Ratty questions about the River Bank, listening attentively to Ratty's warnings about the stoats and weasels of the Wild Wood, not making any comment when his new acquaintance, Otter, suddenly dove for food. He'd even packed up the picnic basket after lunch, although it was much less fun than unpacking it. He'd shown himself the model of animal etiquette, and then he'd literally sunk to the bottom of the River, having lost his balance out of pure selfishness.

But that's not how Ratty sees the incident at all. He laughs as he helps Mole to shore, and tells his friend not to think any more about it. Instead of regretting his hospitality, Ratty extends it further by inviting Mole to stay at his River Bank home. Mole can learn to swim and to row there, Ratty promises, and then he can enjoy the River as much as he wants.

Like a good parent or teacher, Ratty sees Mole's enthusiasm for what it really is—not selfishness or ungratefulness, but an eagerness to learn. Ratty isn't at all angry about the upset boat. After all, as he reminds Mole, he's a Water Rat. What Ratty sees in Mole's irresistible impulse to grab the oars is the beginning of a deep love for the River, and a determination to be part of its life. It's the delight you feel when your very young child suddenly reaches for the book you're reading aloud, grabbing it, wanting to hold it. That's the moment when you know for certain you're raising a reader.

DURING the summer, Mole learns to navigate the River as ably as his teacher, and, with Ratty's guidance, Mole enters the life of the River Bank, meeting and becoming known to all the residents, including the wild and reckless Toad, who is delighted to find a new audience for his bragging accounts of his exploits. As the months pass, Mole grows in assurance and tact, and when winter comes he begins to understand that his new world has an obligation to him in return for his responsibility.

Mole loves his River Bank life, but he won't be satisfied until he's met Badger, the gruff, aristocratic, unself-conscious creature who seems to be an important influence on this world. Badger, Ratty tells him, hates Society—not animals, of course, but the fuss of company. Badger won't respond to a formal invitation, but, Ratty promises, he's certain to be around sometime.

One winter day Mole decides he can't wait anymore, so, in spite of Ratty's warnings, he sets off alone to the Wild Wood to look for Badger, who lives in the middle of that dangerous place. When evening falls, Mole realizes he's utterly lost and, frightened by strange noises and a sense that he's surrounded by stoats and weasels (or perhaps something worse), he huddles fearfully in a hollow tree.

If *The Wind in the Willows* were another kind of story—a fable, perhaps, or a cautionary tale—Mole's unhappy position would be presented as the natural and just result of his willful disobedience, a deserved punishment for not listening to good advice. But this is a magic kingdom, and Mole is the character representing your child. The point is not to prove Mole wrong, but to make things right. And so, the climax of the episode is not a comeuppance, but a plot twist that turns Mole's passivity and self-doubt into action and confidence.

Back home, Ratty, awakened from a nap, realizes that Mole isn't there and guesses correctly where he's gone. With a cudgel and pistol in case of trouble, Ratty heads for the Wild Wood to find his friend. When he does find Mole, still hiding in the hollow tree, Ratty doesn't scold him, say "I told you so," or complain about the inconvenience he's suffered because Mole didn't listen to his warning. Instead, Ratty comforts his frightened friend, even according him a kind of indirect tribute by mentioning that the boastful Toad wouldn't have dared to enter the Wild Wood alone, as Mole did.

After explaining that small animals like themselves shouldn't wander in the Wild Wood alone and unprotected, Ratty starts to lead the way home, and Mole feels as if his company is as much a help to Ratty as Ratty's comfort has been to him. Now that they're on the way home, armed and affording each other safety, Mole sees the trouble he ran into as a simple slipup from overenthusiasm, easily recovered from, just like overturning the boat. It's clear that Mole is, as Winnie-the-Pooh would say, "all right, really."

Even when the two friends are caught in a snowstorm and unable to find their way home, it's Mole who, accidentally, saves the day. Mole's sudden fall over something sharp sets Ratty digging around in the snow. When the cause of Mole's injury—a scraper—is unearthed, Ratty dances for joy, and then starts digging even more energetically. Mole can't figure out why Ratty is so pleased. Ratty shows him a doormat he's found next to the scraper, but Mole can't see its significance—although, by this time, your child is getting the picture. Finally, Ratty brushes the snow away from a brass doorplate to reveal the letters MR BADGER, and Mole finally understands what the excitement is all about. Without knowing it, Mole has found the only safe refuge in the Wild Wood, the house he came to find in the first place.

In this magic kingdom, as in all the others, events conspire to grant the wishes of those who are truly deserving. If Mole is lost and stumbling, he literally trips over the answer to his problem, and at the same time finds his heart's desire. In fact, whenever Mole follows his truest instincts—to climb out of his hole, to seize the oars, to set out by himself into the Wild Wood—he is richly rewarded, because his actions represent the impatience of growth, and growth is the highest value of the magic kingdom, its royal road to success.

But even as it rewards the urgency of Mole's growth, Grahame's magic kingdom offers him another important lesson in making connections. After exhausting himself all day in looking for it, Mole almost passes by Badger's house, and would have missed it entirely, were it not for Ratty. Mole's courage, persistence and luck have brought them to the spot, but it is Ratty's expert reading that lets them know what they've found. Of course, when Ratty scrapes off the last of the snow to reveal the name on the brass plate, Mole can read it as well as Ratty can. Mole is, after all, more grown-up than Pooh or Owl, who still have trouble making the connection between sounds and letters. The connection that Mole has missed is the one between details and a general idea or context.

As your own child's growth into reading teaches you, comprehension goes beyond the basic deciphering of words, and requires logical thinking and an ability to guess at what is not yet shown. Ratty is a past master in this kind of reading, we can see, because he immediately grasps the significance of a scraper in the Wild Wood. While Mole is complaining that someone has stupidly left it there for him to trip over, Ratty sees it as a clue, and starts searching for something that might support his emerging idea that there's a house somewhere near them. When he digs up the doormat, his theory is confirmed, and the name on the plate proves Ratty's hypothesis. Once the brass plate appears, Mole can read it. But Ratty is teaching him that he must also read for meaning by finding and putting together contextual clues. Literally, Mole must learn to dig deeper. Right now, all he can do is stand amazed at Ratty's brilliant analysis, like Dr. Watson after one of Sherlock Holmes's explanations, but Mole will soon learn to connect details and ideas as ably as his teacher.

The way has been long and dangerous, the entrance somewhat mysterious, but once Ratty has shown Mole to Badger's door and the two are safely inside, Mole feels entirely at home. After a hot meal and a sound sleep, Mole takes an opportunity to talk to Badger—something he's been wanting to do since he first arrived in the River Bank—and finds that he can converse with this very aristocratic and influential animal with complete ease, as one sensible underground creature to another. Before, Mole, with Ratty's encouragement, had thought of Badger as somewhat unapproachable. Now he feels accepted by him. In fact, at one point in conversation with Mole and Ratty, Badger stops and deliberately makes clear that the "we" he's speaking of naturally includes Mole. It's a moment of sheer delight for Mole, and for your child, too, since Mole's success represents the success of every child who's trying hard to be a part of the larger world.

Badger's house, in its own way, is as extraordinary as the River itself. The interior seems an idealized combination of country house and castle, with great dining halls equipped with long wooden tables and benches, huge fireplaces, pots shining row after row upon the deep shelves. It extends underground in every direction, how far exactly not even Badger knows, because, as he explains to Mole, he only cleared out the rooms and passages that others had built before him. In the Wild Wood long ago, he tells Mole, there had been a city of rich and powerful people, and his house had formed its foundation. The people and the city had disappeared, but the foundation, which the badgers had taken as their home, remained and flourished. Given this background, it's easy to see why Badger is so very well respected. Besides having descended from the founders of the culture, he is its chief historian and preserver, and, judging from the hungry young hedgehogs eating in his kitchen, a generous benefactor to his smaller neighbors.

Our Mole, it seems, has come a long way from the beginning of the story, from his own "dark and lowly little house" to this ancient, aristocratic, underground mansion. He is justly proud and pleased with his progress, but as he and Ratty trudge home through the snow after their visit with Badger, Mole catches a scent in the winter air and is seized with sudden longing. He implores Ratty to let him follow the scent, but his friend is concentrating on finding the way to the River and won't be delayed. Finally Mole dissolves into tears, and, sobbing, explains to Ratty that they have passed near his old home. Overcome by his friend's sorrow and his own apparent insensitivity, Ratty insists that in spite of the snow and the late hour, they must return to the place where Mole first caught the scent, and find his home.

After a search, Mole finds the scent again and, with Ratty behind him, joyfully dives down the tunnel leading to his underground home, the one he had left so impulsively on a spring morning. Then, suddenly, nostalgia yields to embarrassment. His house, "Mole End," is nothing next to Badger's and can't compare to Ratty's in terms of comfort and style. He has brought his friend here with no chance of dinner or a fire, and made their way home harder than it should have been. Mole apologizes for his impulsiveness, which he sees now as childish weakness, a pointless, selfish yearning for the life he had chosen freely to leave behind.

Once again poor Mole has followed his impulses and seems, at first, to have made a mess of things. Sitting in his narrow hall, he's ashamed of himself, just as he was after he capsized Ratty's boat or got lost in the Wild Wood. But Ratty won't hear of Mole's self-reproach. Instead, Ratty surveys the small house with delight, running about and praising its unique little qualities, and sets to making both of them comfortable. Ratty's good-humored acceptance and excitement overcome Mole's embarrassment, and soon Mole is in high spirits, giving a tour of his house with as much grace and enthusiasm as Badger himself.

Then Mole's neighbors, the field mice, appear at the door, and their caroling tells us that Mole has arrived home at an appropriate and auspicious time. If Mole has any lingering embarrassment about the plainness of his house or the child-like happiness he feels in the old, familiar surroundings, it's dispelled completely by the spirit of Christmas.

In a magic kingdom, the mention of Christmas evokes the possibility of childhood and adulthood coming together as equals through love. It is in itself a magic season, celebrated in classic children's stories for the opportunity it offers to make giving as joyous as receiving, to blend change and tradition effortlessly, to link the simple and the profound. Christmas, then, is the perfect time for Mole to discover that his old home and his new life are both wonderful, and that he doesn't have to reject one to claim the other. Ratty's feast for the singers and the two friends celebrates the union of Mole End and the River Bank, childhood and adulthood, in Mole's life. So Mole's instinct to follow the scent to his old home is rewarded, just as his instincts to climb out of his hole, to grab the oars, or to enter the Wild Wood alone were rewarded. Like the others, this urge represents growth, the impatience to meet a challenge. What awaits Mole at home is one of the last hurdles he must take to adulthood. It is a momentous occasion, because when Mole—or anyone—can acknowledge without embarrassment that childhood lives on in the heart, despite age and experience, then he has really grown up.

When Mole looks at his past and smiles affectionately, we know he's ready for anything the future holds in store for him.

ONCE Mole has celebrated his triumph with a homecoming, Grahame turns our attention to another character who has some growing up to do—the bragging, irresponsible Mr. Toad. Mole represents the good child, the character your own son or daughter can feel close to and identify with. But Toad is just the opposite. Unlike Mole, Toad is rich and well-known, already part of the River Bank world. Yet all his advantages can't give him the quality most prized on the River—stability. Keeping yourself balanced in a boat is, for the River Bank, proof of a personal equilibrium that comes from proper respect for something larger and more powerful than yourself.

Mole learns balance, but only because he realizes its importance, accepts Ratty's help, and works on it regularly. Toad, on the other hand, splashes around awkwardly in a series of boats and refuses to learn how to row properly. Finally, rather than face the challenge of acquiring stability and balance, he leaves the River and takes to the road, with disastrous results. Badger and Ratty despair of him. Toad, it seems, just refuses to grow up.

Mole, as we've seen, tends to be rather too self-conscious and worried about the effects of his actions, and Ratty occasionally has to reassure Mole that he isn't a selfish beast. Toad, in contrast, isn't conscious of anything but what he wants at the moment. Mole may grab at something and then regret his impulsiveness, but Toad, like a selfish child, grabs and then grabs again, without regard to anyone but himself. And like a selfish child, he can't take any real lasting pleasure in something once it's his. Obsessed with one hobby, Toad invariably swears he'll enjoy it for the rest of his life, but soon discards it in favor of his next craze. In just this way, as Ratty tells Mole, Toad has gone through sailing, punting, and houseboating, and despite all this, when Toad goes by in his new, expensive wager-boat, it's clear that he still hasn't learned to row as he should.

The summer morning Ratty and Mole arrive at Toad Hall ready to coach Toad in rowing, Toad has already found a new hobby. He has completely equipped a wooden cart for traveling and declares, as usual, that this delightful pastime will provide him with adventure for the rest of his life. It isn't long before Mole is agog with the prospect Toad enthusiastically paints for him and, despite Ratty's misgivings, by the afternoon they are all off on the open road. After a few days of travel, with Mole and Rat doing most of the work and Toad the eulogizing, the horse and cart end up in a ditch, driven off the road by a speeding motorcar. The trip is ruined, of course—but not for Toad, who immediately switches his obsessive devotion from carts to cars. As soon as the three manage with difficulty to get back to Toad Hall, Toad orders his own large, expensive automobile, vowing with glee to drive into ditches all the contemptible little carts he may find. At last, he declares, he has found the occupation that will make him happy for the rest of his days.

Toad never learns from experience, as Mole does. He lives in an eternal present, changing constantly, always in motion, but never moving forward. Mole comes to the River Bank and finds to his delight that there's a place for him, even a *need* for him. Toad will learn this lesson, too. But unlike Mole, Toad will have to learn it the hard way.

After Toad has had several crashes with several cars, his friends decide that they have an obligation to intervene— "take him in hand," is Badger's way of putting it—for his own good. In this, we've come a long way from Rabbit's attempt in *The House at Pooh Corner* to "unbounce" Tigger. Rabbit's plan was a shortsighted, childish view of how to deal with an annoyance, but the commitment of Badger, Ratty, and Mole to Toad's reformation expresses, in a more grown-up fashion, the responsibility of a community to an individual.

*   *   *

BADGER, Ratty, and Mole appear one morning at Toad Hall and see Toad elaborately dressed for driving, just about to get behind the wheel of yet another expensive car. They stop him abruptly, give orders for the car to be taken away, and march Toad back into his house.

Badger is convinced that Toad can be talked out of his foolishness, so, privately, in another room, Badger gives Toad a severe talking-to. After reducing Toad to repentant sobs, he leads him out in quiet triumph, and announces to Ratty and Mole that their friend has promised never to have anything more to do with cars again. There is a moment of relief, and then Toad recants. He won't give up driving for anything at all, he flatly declares.

Ratty sees that Toad can't be forced *out* of his wild behavior, so he suggests instead that they force him *into* proper behavior. If Toad can't understand the importance and responsibility of being a respectable member of the landed gentry, his friends will stay with him until he does. But until then, as my daughter Franny puts it, Toad is grounded.

The problem is, of course, that nothing—not any kind of punishment—will change Toad unless Toad wants to change. All Ratty manages to do by keeping Toad at home is to prevent him from doing what he wants to do. Once Toad tricks Ratty into leaving him unguarded, he escapes out the window. And once Toad is out from under Ratty's prohibition, he steals the first motorcar he sees. After a short, eventful joyride, Toad is back in captivity, but not at Toad Hall. This time it's prison, and the sentence extends not until he decides to be a good Toad, but for twenty years.

Toad's impulsive journey takes him into the Wide World, outside the magic kingdom of the River Bank and away from the possibility of growth. His luck in the Wide World fluctuates madly, making him wild with conceit at one moment, whimpering in despair the next. His first celebration of freedom lands him in jail, but through what he boastfully regards as his own cleverness, he escapes from prison disguised as a washerwoman, only to find when he reaches a train station that he has no cash for the fare home. Posing as a poor widow who has lost her money, he gets a free ride from the sympathetic engine-driver, but then is forced to jump from the train when pursued by the police.

Toad is elated when he manages to pass himself off as a washerwoman to a bargewoman who offers him a lift to Toad Hall itself, but he is unmasked when she asks for payment in washing and he makes a mess of the laundry. Flung from the barge, Toad dejectedly swims to shore, encumbered by his dress, and then boldly steals the barge horse.

Selling the horse to a gypsy for a few shillings and breakfast further inflates Toad's opinion of his own cleverness. Delighted with himself, literally singing his own praises, he's heading down the road to Toad Hall when suddenly he sees a car approaching. Bursting with conceit, he hails the car and waits to "pitch them a yarn" that he's certain will end in his driving up to Toad Hall in triumph. "That will be one in the eye for Badger!" Toad gloats.

The car slows at his signal, but just as Toad is relishing this lucky end to his prison-break adventures, he recognizes the motorists as the owners of the car he stole. Toad collapses in terror. But Toad's luck has one more good turn in it. The motorists don't recognize him and take him in the car, supposing him to be a washerwoman who fainted in the road.

As they drive to the next town to leave the poor sick woman with friends, Toad regains his nerve and pretends to revive. First, in his washerwoman voice, he begs to sit in the front seat to get some air, and when his request is granted, he asks if he might try to drive a little. They humor the washerwoman, and marvel at her skill behind the wheel.

Then Toad puts on speed, and, gleefully throwing off his disguise and bragging of his exploits, reveals himself as the car thief, escaped from prison. Suddenly the car swerves, crashes through a hedge and into a horse pond. Toad, thrown clear, finds himself flat on his back in a meadow some way off.

Once again Toad dances and sings with joy at his cleverness, until he finds that policemen are pursuing him across the meadow. Desperately he runs from them, not looking where he's going, and falls suddenly into deep rushing water—the River—and the current pulls him along, right down to Ratty's door, where, at last, he finds safety.

so, despite all the bragging and boasting he'll do to his friends afterward, it's really the River itself that finally saves Toad from being captured and sent back to prison. And now that he's back in the River Bank world, just as loud and full of himself as before, he turns all his ridiculous carryings-on into chivalric adventures, until he comes up against something that chastens and humbles him, something he can't change through bluster and bragging.

While he was gone, the stoats and weasels of the Wild Wood have taken Toad Hall. When Toad tries to enter his own house by the road and then by the River, he's stopped, assaulted, and abused by the sentries on guard. No amount of "humbug" or "cleverness" will gain him entrance.

It's an old lesson, and a true one. Toad can't really appreciate what he has until he has lost it. Until now, he's refused to accept the responsibility of his position in River Bank life—he literally runs away from it—but the loss of Toad Hall brings him to his senses, making him realize that he *does* want to return home. And it's the simple fact that Toad wants to grow up that makes it all possible.

THE conclusion of *The Wind in the Willows* presents the comic and heroic retaking of Toad Hall, the driving-off of the stoats and weasels, and the emergence of the new Toad, modest and grown-up. This is where the stories of Mole's social progress and Toad's adventures come together in happy resolution. The young animals each have one more lesson to learn before they can take their places beside Ratty and Badger as adults: Mole has to give help, boldly and independently, and Toad has to accept help, humbly and graciously.

To retake Toad Hall from the Wild Wooders, Badger proposes an invasion strategy to get around the sentries, based on his knowledge of a secret passage under Toad Hall that even Toad himself doesn't know about. If the four friends use the underground passage that leads to the butler's pantry, Badger explains, they can enter the house quietly, surprise the unarmed weasels at dinner, and retake Toad Hall with a minimum of resistance.

Toad eagerly accepts Badger's plan and enthusiastically looks forward to the next night, when the attack will take place. Typically, Toad imagines a glorious role for himself during the conflict and endless adulation afterwards. This, he thinks, will surely be the confirmation of all the heroic, magnificent ideas he's always had about himself.

But all Toad's dreams of glory vanish on the morning of the planned invasion. While Toad is sleeping late, Mole, disguised in the old washerwoman dress, impulsively goes on his own to Toad Hall and plants rumors among the sentries that will assure their desertion at the first sign of trouble. Ratty hears of it and fears that Mole has ruined all their plans. But Mole's instinct is a good one, and the first one he does not regret following. It's a daring move, and so subtle that only the wily Badger realizes its brilliant strategy. Suddenly Mole is the hero, and Toad has to be content with simply going along on the adventure and trying not to get in the way.

When the four friends, heavily armed by Ratty, silently enter the house through the passage, they hear the weasels loudly celebrating in the dining room, the Chief Weasel bragging and singing, just as Toad used to do. The four rush forward and attack the enemy, Toad himself taking on the Chief Weasel, and clear the house of the Wild Wooders in a single sweep. The sentries flee, as Mole had thought they would, and Toad Hall once more belongs to its rightful owner.

Mole's part in the strategy, the battle, and its aftermath is acknowledged by Badger, who praises Mole for his intelligence, skill, and trustworthiness. But the story won't be ended until Toad can join Mole in the world of responsible adults. Toad accomplishes this by quietly and humbly thanking Mole for his cleverness and bravery in retaking Toad Hall—genuinely conceding to his friend the qualities he once foolishly bragged of in himself.

Toad does suffer a brief relapse into his childish behavior, though. Excited by the prospect of a banquet to celebrate his return to Toad Hall, he plans a long evening of speeches and songs, and writes invitations bragging of his adventures and exaggerating his part in the battle with the weasels. When Ratty and Badger intercept the invitations and forbid him to brag and boast at the banquet, Toad agrees with reluctance to obey their order. While Mole writes proper invitations—a responsibility proving his complete social acceptance as an adult—Toad morosely retires to his room to prepare for the evening ahead.

It seems as if, for Toad, growing up is nothing but giving up everything he enjoys. But just as we begin to feel sorry for him, he bursts into one of his boasting songs. Full of conceit, praising his courage, he's the old Toad again—but this time he confines his swaggering to his room, in front of the mirror. He sings the song through twice, imagining a throng of adoring listeners before him, then brushes his hair and goes down to dinner, where he behaves with quiet dignity, warmly greeting his guests, but gently turning aside their praises. His greatest enjoyment that evening is glancing from time to time in the direction of Badger and Ratty, and observing the looks of amazement on their faces. It's a different kind of triumph for Toad, but an entirely satisfying one. He has found his balance at last.

When you read *The Wind in the Willows* with your child, he most closely identifies with "the good Mole," and takes satisfaction from his social success. But Toad's triumph is pleasing, too. And there's something very comforting in the last view we're offered of the four friends strolling through the now peaceable Wild Wood, the mother weasels pointing them out to their babies in admiration and respect. Whether you're as worried as Mole or as careless as Toad when you start out, this ending promises, you *will* grow up, and—although it may seem incredible now—someday the word "children" will come to mean the people who are looking up to *you*.

IN the magic kingdom of the River Bank—as in all the magic kingdoms outside over there—we see that growing up takes both boldness and reserve, the grace to give and to receive help, and the discipline to maintain a balance between the self and the world. In the course of the story, Mole overcomes his hesitancy and Toad his bluster, and each develops a true self-confidence that allows him—like other heroes and heroines of the magic kingdom—to live happily and independently ever after.

It's what you and all of us want more than anything for our own sons and daughters. We all want to give our children the gift of a happy childhood, full of adventure and discovery. The challenge lies in offering the kind of encouragement and help that leads to self-confidence, so that your child can enjoy the growth of independence, conscious of her own strength as well as your support. In a magic kingdom a child's growth happens spontaneously and naturally, but not without the quiet influence of love.

At the very center of *The Wind in the Willows* is a chapter with the mysterious title "The Piper at the Gates of Dawn." It doesn't follow Mole's struggle to figure out River Bank life or Toad's hilarious escapades. Instead, it takes us away from the main plot to tell a separate yet related story of the River Bank, one that reveals the power and magic of the place itself. And what is revealed in this central chapter is a message for you, the parent, about the gift of childhood and your part in it.

Late one evening, Otter confides to Ratty that Portly, Otter's little son, is missing. Ordinarily, Otter wouldn't be too concerned, since Portly is an adventurous and friendly little fellow, who likes wandering around on his own in the safety of the River Bank, where everyone knows and loves him. But it has been several days now, and since Portly isn't a strong swimmer yet, his father worries that he might easily get into trouble in the trickier parts of the River, or be caught in a trap somewhere. Otter tells Ratty he's going to watch for Portly by the ford, an especially loved place where the child had his first swimming lesson. Perhaps, Otter thinks, if Portly passes, he'd stop there to play. Anyway, the father has decided to wait there all night "on the chance."

When Ratty returns home, he tells Mole about Portly, and the two friends, their hearts touched by Otter's anguish, determine to look for the little fellow themselves, by boat and on foot, through the night. Shepard's illustration gives us our most idyllic view of the River, through the trees and reeds, as Ratty and Mole scull in the silent darkness, hoping to find Portly.

Suddenly, Ratty hears something on the wind—the most beautiful piping music he's ever heard—calling to them. Soon Mole hears it, too, and they follow it to a small island in the River, where, just before dawn, the animal-god Pan appears to them. The moment Ratty and Mole recognize the deity and bow in worship, Pan disappears, taking from them the memory of the apparition. They look at each other in mild confusion, and then suddenly see Portly, asleep on the grass before them.

They gently wake Portly, offer him a special treat—a ride in a real boat—and take the child near the ford, where they know his father is waiting. Ratty and Mole leave Portly on the bank, and before they turn to scull away unobserved, they hear the child's excited call to his father and Otter's joyous reply.

As Mole and Ratty row home, they hear the music on the wind again, and this time Ratty can hear words, a beautiful, strange song they can't quite understand, with the refrain "forget, forget." We know that it's the song of Pan, who rescues animals and blesses them with forgetfulness afterward. Ratty repeats for Mole a verse he hears:

> Lest the awe should dwell
> And turn your frolic to fret
> You shall look on my power at the helping hour
> But then you shall forget!

Ratty and Mole don't remember their vision of Pan, but they have unconsciously used the god's own method when they restore Portly to Otter and quietly retreat downriver before they can be discovered. It doesn't really matter where or how Portly was rescued, their actions say, and acknowledgments matter even less. What's important is that Portly is safe and happy, ready to go on adventures again, unfrightened by the world. Everything else, the wind in the willows sings, he will forget.

Like Pan's song in the wind in the willows, like the voice of Ida's father from over the sea, your own voice instills in your child a sense of self-confidence without self-consciousness, the hallmark of a happy childhood, full of adventure and discovery outside over there. When you read with your child, your voice blends with the voice of childhood itself, telling the story of a magic kingdom and the courage and resourcefulness of its child-ruler, growing in wisdom and strength from his own good instincts and common sense. From the miniature landscape of Beatrix Potter, to Christopher Robin's child-sized Forest of nursery friends, and finally to the complex social world of the River Bank, you've helped your child to discover himself, and in doing that, you've begun to help him discover the world.

CHAPTER FOUR

Secret Gardens, Secret Languages

FROM Mr. McGregor's garden in *Peter Rabbit* to the River Bank of *The Wind in the Willows,* your child has traveled far in the land of imagination. A glance at both books, side by side—Potter's child's-hand-sized volumes next to Grahame's novel-length work—will show you the growth and change a few years can accomplish. Imagine, too, the difference in the scope of the fictional landscapes, Potter's encompassing a few country lanes, Grahame's a spreading Arcadia of river, woods, and meadow.

Each magic kingdom opens on a wider world than the one before, with more complex problems and concerns, to match your child's growing interests, but in each the same heroic adventure is accomplished: a character explores a new world, faces its dangers, and triumphs through courage and common sense. By sharing both the challenges and the rewards of the magic kingdom's hero in imagination, your child grows in independence and self-confidence, learning to face the adventures of his own life and becoming the hero of his own childhood.

Like the Forest of Arden in Shakespeare's comedies, a magic kingdom is a place far from distractions, where true character can emerge and become known, free from the normally inhibiting restrictions of ordinary life. The country fields of Beatrix Potter, Wonderland's gardens and landscapes, Christopher Robin's Forest, and the green River Bank by their very nature offer the possibility of freedom and growth, and so do the jungle of Kipling's Mowgli stories, the secret garden in Frances Hodgson Burnett's classic tale, and Neverland, Narnia, and the Land of Oz. All these magic kingdoms take the form of gardens—places set apart for the cultivation of young life, a natural landscape where the essential self can blossom and grow.

* * *

THE garden in the magic kingdom is a metaphor for that secret part of identity that is childhood itself, and growth here is mysterious and unobservable. In the transitions from infancy to childhood to young adulthood, it seems that, like a seed, the self needs quiet and isolation in order to grow. Long times of quiescence, when change appears to slow down or stop, are followed by dramatic growth, culminating in adolescence. At these crucial times, when your child is learning so much about himself and the world, the magic kingdom offers the garden as an imaginary place of solitude and contemplation, a retreat in preparation for the next advance.

It's not surprising, then, that after Alice arrives so unexpectedly in Wonderland and later in the Looking-Glass World, her first concern is to find her way into a garden, to rest and to think about what's happened to her. It's quite in the nature of the secret garden that Alice must begin to solve the riddle of the world she's found herself in before she can enter these gardens.

And once in, Alice discovers that the Garden of Live Flowers in the Looking-Glass World and the Queen's Garden in Wonderland are as full of paradoxes, conflict, and unreason as any other place she's found. Neither garden is a comfortable haven of rest and ease; each is a field of challenge, where Alice must stay alert and awake, like the Live Flowers, who scorn their earthly cousins because they spend time sleeping instead of talking.

In the same way, Beatrix Potter's landscapes offer gardens, like Mr. McGregor's, where Peter Rabbit, first alone and then with his cousin Benjamin, tests his courage. The result of his garden adventure seems at first to be a big setback for Peter's independence—after all, he's terribly frightened, becomes ill, and is even punished for it. But when we see Peter all grownup, in *The Tale of the Flopsy Bunnies,* he's got a fine garden of his own, and is so successful that he can give part of what he grows to his little nieces and nephews. His scolding Uncle Benjamin and Mr. McGregor may have thought at the time that they'd taught him a lesson about obedience, but it's the garden that really teaches him, and that lesson is all about growth.

And so it is with Christopher Robin. Whenever he opens his green door to step into the Forest, he's also entering a garden. Here he tends lovingly to his friends, gently putting right what's tangled, removing anything harmful, seeing to their needs. By caring for others, like a good gardener, Christopher Robin grows himself, just as Wendy does in Neverland, by watching over Peter Pan and the Lost Boys in their tree house.

Sometimes the surprise of a gardenlike, green countryside after dull surroundings works magically to change a growing character. Mole's first view of the grasses and willows by the River Bank opens his eyes to the joy of the world above ground. Dorothy Gale, accustomed to the gray Kansas prairie, is filled with wonder by the verdant beauty of Oz and the possibilities of life in a magic kingdom. And a garden can offer a mystery, too. How else can a single walled garden contain all of Narnia? How does a gardener restore to life all of Middle-earth?

At its most powerful, a secret garden can welcome in a lost child, homeless and friendless, and after time restore that child to the world happy, confident, resourceful, and full of hope. This is the story of Mary Lennox, of Frances Hodgson Burnett's classic *The Secret Garden,* and of Mowgli, the man-cub of Rudyard Kipling's Jungle Books. Both children, having lost their homes and families, find their way alone into the garden of a magic kingdom—Mary, the walled rose garden on the Yorkshire moors, and Mowgli, the jungle of India. Both discover within the garden, and within themselves, what they need most. They face the challenge of growth, and leave their secret gardens as child-heroes, rulers of the magic kingdom.

IN the secret garden, change *does* occur, though it may be imperceptible from the outside. Inwardly, your child experiments with identity by imagining himself in another's place, feeling and thinking through possibilities. A prelude to the emergence of a new self, this inner change needs talking over, and because the whole process is internal, the language of the conversation must be private, a secret code to express inwardly what cannot yet be expressed to others.

At the same time, children who are growing up are always facing the challenges of the secret languages of the adult world—the expressions and the gestures of social life. In the Forest, Christopher Robin struggles with reading and writing, until at last he masters the very grown-up art of polite correspondence, and writes a letter his friends can understand. And in the Jungle, Mowgli sets his mind to learning the Master Words, a kind of jungle etiquette that expresses in speech the conventions of animal society. The purpose of Christopher Robin's writing and Mowgli's Master Words is to acknowledge and strengthen the bonds between friends, and by learning these secret languages, the world will be safer and happier for the growing children.

These are the secret languages children learn and grow into, but there's another secret language that is a spontaneous, natural expression of childhood, when nature and imagination seem part of each other, and inseparable from a child's sense of wonder. Babies start out speaking this natural language fluently, Mary Poppins explains, but forget it as they grow. Dickon, the country boy in *The Secret Garden,* has found a way to retain his childlike ability to be part of nature itself and can understand all the animals and birds on the moor, and even "speak robin." And *Peter Pan* gives your own child a chance to recover the power of this secret language. Fairies are born, Peter tells Wendy, with a baby's first laugh, but it is only the grown children listening to the story who can save Tinkerbell by expressing their belief in imagination.

It is in the stories of the magic kingdom, the stories you're reading now with your child, that the secret language of the adult world and the secret language of childhood join to create an imaginary place like the Forest, the River Bank,

Neverland and Wonderland. And the purpose of this magic place, where dreams and waking life can come together, is to prepare for the world outside by meeting the most important challenge, growth. Growth is the message carried in whispers by the wind in the willows, and growth is the meaning of the secret language, and of the magic that awaits your child in the secret garden.

LIKE the language of dreams, the secret language of the secret garden is the way your child talks to herself about her hopes and fears as she faces the future. And stories of secret gardens are themselves like dreams, where the isolated self can connect with an imagination shared by all of us. It may be that this secret language can't be translated literally or entirely, but its meaning mysteriously penetrates nevertheless.

When Alice finds a book in the Looking-Glass World, she knows instinctively she has to hold it up to the mirror to read it, but even then the strange Looking-Glass language keeps the meaning of the poem "Jabberwocky" tantalizingly elusive. The story of the brave son who slays the monster Jabberwock, Alice ponders, "seems to fill my head with ideas— only I don't exactly know what they are!"

"*Somebody* killed *something*" is the extent of her interpretation in words, but Tenniel's illustration, which shows us what Alice is imagining as she reads, makes it clear that she understands the poem far better than she knows. The monster "whiffling" and "burbling" toward us is a fully realized creature, right down to the long, menacing "claws that catch."

When you look at this illustration with your child, notice who it is standing between you and that "manxome foe," the Jabberwock, ready to stop the creature with a "vorpal blade." As your child can see, Alice has imagined herself—in appropriate medieval clothing—as the hero of the poem, the young warrior who faces the Jabberwock, conquers it, and returns home triumphant.

Later in the story of the Looking-Glass World, Alice gets a lecture on the literal meaning and etymology of some of the difficult words in the poem from Humpty Dumpty. The translation is fun, like a decoding game, and Alice finds she can join in after a while. But the way to the heart of meaning is still the path of imagination, as we see when Alice pictures the "toves" "gyring and gimbling" in their secret garden home.

If Humpty Dumpty boasts that he can explain "all the poems that were ever invented," it's clear by the end of the chapter, when "all the king's horses and all the king's men" rush by Alice on the way to the disaster that she—and your child—has anticipated, that Alice's way of understanding is truer than Humpty's. Alice can imagine herself into a poem and discover its meaning, but Humpty Dumpty's method prevents him from understanding the real significance of *any* poem, even the one that's all about him. Confronted with a mystery in a secret language, Alice, and your child, rises to the occasion. All Humpty Dumpty can do is fall.

FOR all his bluster and bragging, Humpty Dumpty can't match Alice in imagination, comprehension, or judgment. And these advantages—a natural part of Alice revealed through the challenges she meets in Wonderland and the Looking-Glass World—represent the greatest power within the magic kingdom, where a child's own innate sense of what's true and what's important is always affirmed.

Helping your child to grow means preparing him to face the world outside his home with confidence, optimism, and enthusiasm. You know that your child can tell what's right, and, when the time comes, will do the right thing.

You can help him to become aware of this through imagination, by offering him stories in which a young character enters a new world and faces its challenges successfully. In identifying with this character, your child imagines himself acting boldly, with confidence, taking responsibility, and defending his principles.

[89]

In a secret garden, a child can find this power within himself and use it by himself, alone and apart from public view. What a child learns about the exercise of his own power in this little world will prepare him for the larger one, outside the walls of the secret garden.

ALICE stands up for common sense and truth in Wonderland, and in the Forest, Christopher Robin gives his attention to helping his friends out of their difficulties, which are usually caused by confusion or misunderstanding. The ability to see with greater understanding makes Christopher Robin monarch of all he surveys, and he uses his power wisely and responsibly for the benefit of each of the animals in the Forest and the happiness of the whole little community of friends. And though the children of secret gardens express their power differently, they always use it for good, interceding when necessary.

When Owl's tree house is blown down by a storm, everyone in the Forest joins in helping him to recover his belongings and search for a new place to live. Even Eeyore, in an uncharacteristically social mood, looks about the Forest, and when he finds what he thinks is "just the house for Owl," he leads Piglet, Pooh, and Christopher Robin to it with a certain amount of pride.

Eeyore *should* be proud, because he's worked hard to solve a problem for a friend. It's just that the house he proposes for Owl already has a tenant—Piglet, who is suddenly put in a terribly awkward position. Although pained, Piglet gives up his house to Owl, without telling Eeyore what a sacrifice he's making. But Eeyore senses that something's wrong, and he asks, "What do *you* think, Christopher Robin?"

Now Christopher Robin could explain to Eeyore that he's made a mistake; that the house, although a fine one, is Piglet's. But if he did that, he'd be embarrassing the retiring Eeyore, who might, as a result, decide never to go out on a limb for anyone for any reason ever again. He'd also be undoing Piglet's noble, selfless action, a sacrifice which was undertaken freely. If Christopher Robin simply spoke the plain truth at this point, he'd be preventing two generous acts of helpfulness, and Owl *still* wouldn't have a home.

It's a time when Christopher Robin has the opportunity to shape the growth of the friends who depend upon him, by either stopping or, in some way, encouraging their attempts to help each other. In a moment of inspiration, he answers Eeyore's question with one of his own. What does Piglet think *he* would do, if he'd lost his home, as Owl has?

"He'd come and live with me," Pooh replies readily, spontaneously joining in the spirit of generosity, and Piglet accepts the invitation with as much delight as relief. And so after a disaster that leaves a friend without a home, and a mistake that threatens to evict another one, the Forest community is united by a single vision of the common good, under Christopher Robin's wise influence. This is Christopher Robin's last act as ruler of his magic kingdom, before he must leave the Forest for the schoolroom. His resolution of the problem brings out the best in each of his closest friends, leaving the circle even closer than before.

It's a story that brings us back to the source of Milne's writing—his son Christopher's play with the stuffed animals, the boy speaking for each in conversations, bringing them to life with imagination. You've seen your own child play this way, too, using figures or toys to act out a situation, talking for different characters, walking them around on a table or the floor. And often these impromptu stories dramatize the resolution of a problem or misunderstanding, ending a conflict between two characters, and getting them back to being friends again.

In imaginative play, your child tries on the role of the peacemaker, the one who can see the way to solve a problem and still save everyone's feelings. Like Christopher Robin, your child feels responsible for his toy friends, and practices compromise and conciliation in the private language of play. The *Pooh* books acknowledge your child's growing interest in a social world, and encourage him to imagine himself not just taking part, but ruling wisely and well, as Christopher Robin rules in the secret garden of his magic kingdom.

TO be the wise and good ruler, to use power to help others, is the hopeful dream of every young heart. These stories of the magic kingdom were written during a time when Britain's power and influence extended throughout the world. In these stories for children, we can find the best intentions and the most exciting adventures of the British Empire, ageless and unchanged from the childhood of our modern world.

And for the British, India was the secret garden of the Empire. Despite the fact that Canada, Australia, parts of Africa, and the Middle East were all just as much under Britain's control, the idea of the Empire, especially its exotic, romantic qualities, came to be identified most strongly with the subcontinent. Victoria was Queen of England, but she was Empress of India, a fact Parliament made official after some debate in 1876. And India itself was, in the evocative phrase, the jewel in the crown—rare, rich, beautiful.

India's civilization had flourished thousands of years before England existed, and its ancient, timeless culture fascinated the British. Indian artifacts, silks, and cuisine were all highly valued in London, and a preference for Indian over Chinese tea was regarded as a mark of good breeding. It was as if acquiring something from the subcontinent would give the owner a part of its mystery.

But India never yielded to definition. It remained, for the British, an area on the map that seemed almost a land of imagination, a place preserved, ageless and changeless, from the childhood of the world. India was a secret garden with a high wall around it, and to the British—even those who lived on the subcontinent—essentially an imperial enigma.

The British who lived and worked in India led a life apart, sequestered in their own social territory, even developing their own language of sorts, a casual mixture of some Hindustani and English that expressed their cultural position exactly. An informal, insider's lingo, made to be spoken rather than written, it was a slapdash slang that sprang up of necessity, as a way of talking about the Raj—that is, British rule in India—from the British point of view.

A young journalist, Rudyard Kipling, was the first to bring this language to the page, using its expressions in his stories and poems as a way of representing daily life among the British in India. In writing of the Raj in its own secret language, so to speak, Kipling brought a reflection of British life in India not only to the small British community on the subcontinent, but also to their fascinated countrymen at home, always curious about ordinary, day-to-day life in an exotic place.

The keenest pleasure in reading Kipling's poems and stories, C. S. Lewis remarked, is feeling that somehow you are a part of the small, privileged society he describes. Through the secret language of the Raj, Kipling gratifies our desire "to belong, to be inside, to be in the know."

RUDYARD Kipling was born in Bombay in 1865, the son of John Lockwood Kipling, a professor who served as the curator of the Lahore Museum, and Alice Macdonald, whose family was among the elite in the very small circle of power in London. Two of Kipling's uncles were famous Pre-Raphaelite painters, and his cousin, Stanley Baldwin, would one day be prime minister.

At the age of five, Kipling's parents brought him to England with his three-year-old sister, Trix, and, in accordance with the well-established tradition of British India, the children were boarded with a family in order to go to school while their parents returned to their life in India.

From his childhood, then, Kipling was of two worlds—one British, one Indian—and he knew the challenges of passing from one to the other alone. After attending a boys' school called by the colorful name Westward Ho! which later inspired the comic misadventures of *Stalky and Co.*, Kipling returned to the subcontinent in 1882 as a journalist, writing about the British in India.

And it was this cultural frontier, where modern Britain met ancient India, that inspired Kipling's most successful work. Even after Kipling had returned with his family to live in England, he continued to write about the outposts of the Empire, delighting his readers with *Kim,* the story of an Anglo-Indian boy coming of age against a background of international intrigue, and the *Just So Stories,* which created the illusion of Indian and African fables rendered in English, tales told in a British nursery to a young child before bed.

The language, the values, the struggles of this time and place afforded Kipling ample material, which he drew on even during a long stay in Vermont, beginning in 1892, while living with his American wife's family. It was here that he wrote *The Jungle Book* and *The Second Jungle Book,* stories of Mowgli, a boy who wanders into a wolves' lair and is raised to young manhood in the Indian jungle.

Mowgli first made his appearance as part of the short story "In the Rukh," which Kipling wrote with adults in mind rather than children. In this story, Mowgli is grown-up, and astounds a British resident when he suddenly walks out of the jungle dressed only in a loincloth and crowned with a wreath of flowers, a living image of man untouched by civilization.

And Mowgli seems to have come upon Kipling himself just as unexpectedly, because a year later the writer returned to the story of the young man of the jungle. This time Kipling determined to begin the tale of Mowgli from the beginning, and to tell the story for children.

WHEN you first open Kipling's Jungle Books, you and your child will probably be reminded of Kenneth Grahame's magic kingdom. After all, both the Jungle and the River Bank are natural landscapes where animals have the same social awareness as people, and, like good parents and teachers, do their best to help a newcomer to understand and to live within the conventions of their civilized life.

The difference between these magic kingdoms is a matter of purpose. Mole's needs are not Mowgli's, and although both child-heroes are on the path of growth, it will lead them in different ways.

The River Bank of *The Wind in the Willows* is a landscape of imagination entirely populated by animals, and the challenge Mole faces as he enters its social world one fine spring day is the sometimes difficult business of fitting in, of belonging, and of making a place for himself. The River Bank has much to teach, and a great part of Mole's growth involves listening to its social codes, genially explained by Ratty, and then behaving in accordance with them.

Mole accomplishes his social goal admirably, finding that his own inclinations are usually a good guide to proper behavior. By the end, Mole is unquestionably at home in the River Bank, a cosmopolitan animal moving gracefully in his wide social world, but deep down, we know, the same old Mole.

The Jungle of Mowgli's story is a different matter, because however the boy loves it, the Jungle's social world and its laws are not made with him in mind. Simply, the Jungle cannot be Mowgli's home as the River Bank is Mole's. Mowgli's challenge in the Jungle is not to create a place for himself, but to create *himself*, his own uniquely human character.

The Jungle has much to teach Mowgli in its way, but learning its lessons will require more than understanding and acceptance. To grow in this magic kingdom, Mowgli has to absorb the wisdom of the Jungle, and then distill it into a personal code, one that will apply to him—the only human—alone.

THE *Jungle Book* opens with an account of how Mowgli came to live in the jungle. Because he's a human in the Jungle, Mowgli is unique—just like your own child—and his challenge lies in discovering how the rules he learns apply to him.

The story begins with a description of a father and mother wolf and their cubs in their lair; they are as sympathetic and articulate as an ordinary human family. The father wolf is readying himself to go hunting in the early evening, when he finds to his annoyance that Shere Khan, the tiger, is hunting in the area and frightening all the game.

Suddenly, the tiger's quarry appears at the mouth of the wolves' lair—a "man-cub," a little boy just old enough to walk. Mother and Father Wolf are surprised to see a human child so close, and marvel when he shows no fear of them, but looks into their faces, laughs, and then begins to nurse with the wolf cubs.

When Shere Khan demands the man-cub as his lawful prey, Mother Wolf angrily refuses to give the child up. She orders the tiger to leave, and predicts that one day the man-cub will hunt Shere Khan himself. The tiger withdraws, darkly insisting that he will get his quarry in the end. But Mother Wolf has decided that the man-cub, whom she calls "Mowgli" (meaning "frog"), will be raised with her own cubs and learn to run and to hunt with their Pack, as a wolf and one of the Free People of the Jungle.

After his formal acceptance by the Council, Mowgli becomes a wolf of the Seeonee Pack and a member of the Free People of the Jungle. Like his brother wolves, he must learn from Baloo the Bear the Law of the Jungle and the Master Words, a secret language of survival that enables a cub to protect himself among all the Jungle's people. And because the panther, Bagheera, has special knowledge of the world of men, having escaped from captivity, he, too, will educate Mowgli. Together, the bear and the panther come to regard their pupil as "our man-cub," and Mowgli relies upon them not only for guidance and instruction, but for love and support as well.

The Jungle, then, is more than just a wild, fascinating playland where Mowgli will have adventures. It's a magic kingdom, a place where Mowgli will grow and learn what he must to meet the challenges ahead of him—to face Shere

Khan in combat and to reenter the world of men. Like Alice, Christopher Robin, and the rest, Mowgli's experience in this magic kingdom will prepare him for the larger world outside, giving him the confidence to take on whatever life has to offer.

BUT the Jungle is a magic kingdom with greater dangers than you and your child have seen so far. Mowgli and his friends have a more difficult game to play, with higher stakes, than do Christopher Robin and his animal toys that come to life. In the Forest, everyone is a friend, and the challenge lies in making this simple, happy truth apparent to those who don't see it.

In the Jungle, though, there are friends and there are enemies, predators, and prey, and Mowgli must learn to recognize and to deal with each according to the Law of the Jungle. And the situation is further complicated by the fact that Mowgli is a man-cub, the only one of his kind in the Jungle.

This doesn't mean that he is in charge, like Christopher Robin. Instead, it means that Mowgli will have to make his own way, alone. Baloo acknowledges this when he decides to teach Mowgli *all* the Jungle Law, not just the part applying to the wolf pack.

No one can tell what dangers and opportunities Mowgli may meet, and no one can be sure what qualities he may be able to draw upon. If he is to grow to his potential, Baloo reasons, he must know everything the Jungle can teach him. When Mowgli is fluent in the letter of the Jungle Law, then he can extract its spirit, the source of its meaning, and find what he needs to create himself.

What you and your child will find as you read the Jungle Books together is that the Law Baloo teaches Mowgli has real meaning in the world of people, too. In the Jungle Books, you'll see and hear the values of the magic kingdom named and discussed clearly and openly, where, in other stories, they remain unspoken but implicit.

"Wisdom, Strength, and Courtesy" will guide Mowgli

through life, whether in the Jungle or the Man-Village. This is the way Mowgli faces the challenge of Shere Khan's thirst for blood, and, by outwitting him, becomes master of the jungle, ruler of the magic kingdom.

FIRST Mowgli must learn the Law and all the Master Words—a special royal education in acknowledgment of his unique identity. Mowgli learns quickly, and Baloo proudly shows off his pupil to Bagheera by having Mowgli recite the Master Words "We be of one blood, ye and I," in the languages of the four-footed animals, birds, and snakes.

By the age of twelve, Mowgli hunts with the best of his Pack and keeps the Jungle Law faithfully. In fact, the man-cub thinks of himself as a wolf, like his brothers, and has come to believe that he, too, was born in the Jungle. But at this crucial age, on the verge of adolescence, the challenge of Shere Khan will bring Mowgli to a closer sense of his real identity.

It is a dangerous time in the Seeonee Wolf Pack. Akela, the venerable leader of the wolves, has missed his prey, and, according to Law, must now defend his position against all younger wolves who would replace him. Shere Khan takes advantage of this uncertainty to turn the Pack against Mowgli, who has risen in power among the wolves and stands almost on a par with Akela himself. Mocking the Pack for following an old wolf and a man-cub, Shere Khan tells them to kill Akela and give him Mowgli for his prey. Isn't it true, he sneers, that none of them dares look Mowgli in the eye?

Mowgli's ability to stare down any animal in the Jungle—a magic power that Max of *Where the Wild Things Are* also possesses and uses to tame the creatures he meets—represents the first proof that the man-cub really is different from the wolves and the rest of the People of the Jungle. Why should the Free People trust him, Shere Khan asks, since he isn't of the Jungle, but of the Man-Village?

Akela defends Mowgli, arguing that although he's a man-cub, he has nevertheless lived under the Jungle Law, "our brother in all but blood," and has earned the Pack's protection. But Shere Khan's insistence that Mowgli is different convinces the majority of the Pack to cast out Mowgli and to condemn his defender to death.

At this terrible moment—thrown out of the only brotherhood he has ever known and forced to watch the humiliation of a dearly loved mentor and friend—Mowgli rises to the challenge. If the Pack rejects him for being different, Mowgli is about to show what the difference between them really means.

Taking some of the "Red Flower"—fire—that terrifies everyone in the Jungle except him, Mowgli acknowledges that he is human with a show of his power. He brandishes the flame before the cowering Pack, saves Akela's life, and singes Shere Khan with the torch, shaming the tiger. Then, with the oath that he will someday return and lay his enemy's hide on Council Rock, Mowgli leaves the Jungle for the Man-Village.

It's a victory, but not an entirely happy one for Mowgli. He has saved Akela from death, yet the man-cub is still cast out of the Pack, and, except for the few wolves who remained with him, has no brothers to hunt with. He must go to the Man-Village now, out of necessity rather than choice, not knowing what awaits him or how he will be received. The thought of it makes Mowgli weep for the first time in his life.

WHEN Mowgli goes to the Man-Village, he's recognized as the son that his mother, Messua, lost to a tiger years before, and Messua treats him with kindness and affection. But Messua is the only person in the Man-Village who makes a favorable impression on Mowgli. The rest strike him as silly, greedy, hypocritical, and superstitious. Still, the Law of the Jungle, which he abides by even in the Man-Village, requires that Mowgli bear their absurdities with patience.

As his job, Mowgli is sent out to watch the herds and drive them home at the end of the day. It's a boring task that even the least adventurous child could accomplish, but Mowgli uses the opportunity to capture and kill his enemy, Shere Khan. With the help of Akela and Gray Brother, Mowgli traps the tiger at the bottom of a ravine and stampedes the herds down to trample him.

But when Mowgli goes to work with the wolves to skin the tiger, he is interrupted by the chief hunter of the village, a man named Buldeo. Buldeo wants the skin for himself, and tries to manipulate Mowgli into giving it to him. Mowgli continues his work and refuses Buldeo, explaining that he had a long-standing score to settle with this particular tiger. When Buldeo persists, Mowgli calls to Akela to push the man away.

Astounded by this mysterious boy who talks of vendettas with tigers and has wolves who obey his orders, Buldeo decides that he is seeing some kind of sorcery. "Maharaj! Great King!" he whispers with reverent fear to Mowgli, who responds with an amused, "Yes."

Mowgli continues to skin the tiger while Buldeo runs to the village with the embroidered tale of magic and sorcery. When dusk falls and the hide is off the tiger, Mowgli drives home the herd, only to find half the village waiting for him, bells ringing and lights ablaze. At first, Mowgli thinks they are congratulating him for the kill, but they stone him instead, crying that he is a demon, a wizard, and a wolf's cub. Mowgli, cast out of the Jungle for being a man, is now driven out of the village for being a wolf.

"I am two Mowglis," the man-cub sings at Council Rock, "but the hide of Shere Khan is under my feet." As a child fast becoming an adult Mowgli triumphs, acknowledged as the king of the magic kingdom, yet he is still between the two worlds of the Jungle and the Man-Village. In the years to come he must discover the Mowgli within him, the essential self that unites the human and the natural, so he can follow the path that is his alone.

* * *

IN *The Second Jungle Book,* Mowgli learns more about man, this time from the relative safety of the Jungle. What he discovers convinces him that man can be dangerous, foolish, destructive, and vain. And the comparison of Mowgli with the men he meets makes clear to your child what an extraordinary difference the man-cub's upbringing in his magic kingdom has made in him.

In "The King's Ankus," Mowgli finds a jeweled elephant goad among the treasures guarded by a cobra below the ruins of an ancient city. He takes the goad away with him out of curiosity, and is puzzled by the cobra's warning that it will bring death. When he shows the jeweled goad to Bagheera and learns its cruel purpose in disciplining elephants, he throws it away in disgust, thinking he has ended its deadly power. But, as Mowgli finds, its power has only now been released.

To the Jungle-bred Mowgli, raised in the magic kingdom, the ankus is only a heavy, glittering object whose use is bloody and vicious. But to men, Bagheera tells him, its value is worth killing for many times.

And, accordingly, when Mowgli looks in the place where he left the jeweled goad, he finds it is gone, carried away by a man. Tracking with Bagheera, Mowgli traces the meeting and endings of several trails, and discovers the bodies of murdered men. By the time he sees the ankus again, six have died trying to get or keep the treasure, so Mowgli wisely returns the jeweled goad to the cobra, where its power can kill no more.

What Mowgli learns about the men he observes shows him—and your child—how different the man-cub is from other humans. Mowgli is not tempted by wealth or power, he is able to distinguish lies from the truth, and he can be relied on for courageous action. His magic kingdom, the Jungle, has kept him from learning the faults of men, and so he is through and through what a child is at heart—intelligent, capable, and loyal to those who show love.

* * *

IN Mowgli's last great challenge as one of the Free People of the Jungle, he saves his Pack from the dhole, vicious hunting dogs, savages who do not keep the Jungle Law. The story "Red Dog" shows how Mowgli has grown to combine the strongest traits of both the man-cub and the wolf when facing an enemy. Using both his intellect and his superior physical strength, Mowgli, with the help of Kaa (the Rock Python), taunts the dhole pack into chasing him, and brings them directly in the deadly path of the Little People of the Jungle—the bees, whom no animal can fight.

Along the way, Mowgli tells himself, he will use his unique identity to the pack's advantage. First, he'll chatter insults to the dholes from a tree, like a monkey; then he'll run like a deer; and, at last, after the bees have routed the dholes, he'll face any remaining dholes as "Mowgli the Man," fighting them with his long knife.

Mowgli vanquishes the dhole pack with the strength of all the Jungle Law that has been instilled in him by his training, but Akela is mortally wounded in the fight. At his death, Akela declares that Mowgli has paid his debt to the Pack that saved his life. Now, Akela insists, Mowgli must return to his own people. "Who will drive me?" demands the man-cub, and Akela, dying, whispers, "Mowgli will drive Mowgli."

AKELA's prophecy comes true when Mowgli is seventeen. With spring in the air, all the People of the Jungle are busy beginning life in the new year. To his surprise, Mowgli finds himself "drawn by both feet" to man again. He walks out of the Jungle, crowned with a wreath of jasmine, truly a ruler of a magic kingdom.

Seeing him approach, Messua presents her baby son— Mowgli's brother—and begs a royal blessing. Will Mowgli grant the child "the Favor of the Jungle," so that the magic he possesses will be passed on?

Mowgli senses the connection between himself and his own people—especially Messua, and later, a young woman he sees for a moment—but he also mourns the loss of the Jungle as his home. His growth has made the change inevitable, yet, as Kaa sympathizes, "It is hard to cast the skin."

Again, Mowgli weeps, feeling the pain of separation and the uncertainty of a new, unfamiliar life. But we are confident that he is ready to face the world and triumph in it, strengthened by a royal education and with Gray Brother, one of the wolves of his old lair, by his side. Mowgli must leave the Jungle, but the Jungle will never leave Mowgli, your child sees, as the man and wolf go off together to seek their own trail in the world that is waiting outside.

FOR the British, India represented the unchanging world of ancient, mysterious truths, where the boundaries we assume between spirit and body, animals and people, this world and the next, seemed somehow to disappear, or at least become passable. Novelist Wilkie Collins thrilled the public with *The Moonstone,* a story of hypnosis and other mysteries regarded as characteristically Indian. The last story Charles Dickens was writing before his death, the uncompleted *Mystery of Edwin Drood,* also depended on Britain's fascination with Indian cults and their strange powers over life and death.

Even the cliché of the turbaned snake charmer playing a flute before an entranced cobra, or the mystic lying on a bed of nails, expresses the Western perception of India as a land where impossible things can happen. If there is any place on earth where we could leave behind the trappings of modern life and enter a world where truths can be revealed, it must be India. For the British, India was the land of imagination, and, because they imagined truth to be at its heart, it was also a magic kingdom.

Mowgli's magic kingdom is the Jungle, the place he comes upon as if led there by fate, where he learns wisdom, strength, and courtesy in preparation for his life in the Man-

[103]

Village. All of the characteristics that the British associated with the subcontinent—mystery, ancient truth, exotic powers—are present in the Jungle, and Mowgli's education makes it possible for him to bring this magic with him to the world outside, to guide and to strengthen him in adult life. The lessons he learns, the confidence he finds through meeting the challenges of the magic kingdom, stay with him, just as they do with Alice, Christopher Robin, Mole, and all the rulers of magic kingdoms who inspire your child's imagination.

IF India holds within it the magic of a secret garden, then a secret garden—even one in England—can hold some of the magic of India. In Frances Hodgson Burnett's *The Secret Garden,* your child finds Mary Lennox, born in India of British parents. At the age of nine Mary is orphaned and sent to live with her morose and eccentric uncle at Misselthwaite Manor in Yorkshire. Mary is a thoroughly spoiled and uncaring child, and seems condemned to remain so, but once she is in Yorkshire she begins to change. Mary discovers a walled rose garden at the Manor—a forgotten place that emanates magic. The secret garden draws Mary in and helps her to discover the mysterious connections between mind and body, present and past, dreams and reality.

At Misselthwaite, Mary's curiosity is aroused by a servant's offhand remark about a walled rose garden that has been locked up for ten years. Unaccustomed to secrets and challenges, and intrigued by the idea of a garden that is closed to her, Mary determines to find an entrance and to see it for herself.

Through what she describes as a kind of "Magic," Mary discovers the key and the door to the garden. First keeping the secret, then sharing it with a new friend, Dickon, Mary brings the neglected garden—and herself—back to life and growth. Later, she shares the secret garden with her cousin, Colin, an invalid child who is as spoiled as Mary used to be, and together they cultivate the growth of the garden and each other. In the end, the once-sickly Colin is returned to health and is happily reunited with his father, Mary's uncle, who is himself reborn into joy through the magic of the secret garden.

The purpose of the secret garden, like all magic kingdoms, is not to provide a place for fantasy and dreaming, but to prepare a child for reality and growth. When Mary enters the secret garden for the first time, she looks around in wonder at this "secret kingdom" that seems to be "a world all her own," but then she literally gets down to earth, dropping to her knees to weed, and instinctively begins to transform the neglected garden, as well as herself.

Like learning to read and write in Christopher Robin's Forest or becoming aware of social responsibilities in Mole and Ratty's River Bank, Mary's weeding, pruning, and planting here in the secret garden represent a special challenge that must be faced to ensure growth. And because the secret garden works as both symbol and reality, the work of the garden has a double purpose.

By cultivating the garden, which had been neglected for the last ten years, Mary—the neglected ten-year-old child—clears the ground and prepares the soil for her own growth as well. When Mary learns how to weed, hoe, and water to help beautiful plants to grow, when she learns to accept advice and help gratefully from a friend who knows about flowers, and when she willingly shares her secret with another child who needs its magic, then she's succeeded in saving herself as well as the garden.

BURNETT explained that the inspiration for *The Secret Garden* came from her own experience coaxing back to life a walled rose garden at Maytham Hall in Kent, where she lived from 1898 to 1907. Certainly the garden gave her a metaphor that included both the irresistible energy for growth and the need for help and encouragement—sun, water, and room enough to flower.

Perhaps more than any other author, Burnett works the

elements of the magic kingdom tradition literally into her story. Mary doesn't have to imagine or dream her magic kingdom into existence, as Alice does, because the actual garden is right there, waiting for her discovery. And because the garden is part of the manor grounds, it seems both far and near, like all magic kingdoms, suddenly and magically revealing its key and door to her through nature itself.

Before *The Secret Garden* was published in 1911, Burnett was already famous as a children's author because of the immense popular success of *Little Lord Fauntleroy* (1886) and *A Little Princess* (1905), which established the cult of the "Beautiful Child." The theme of both stories, widely imitated at the time, is the assumption that children ought to remain the same—passively good—rather than changing and growing.

Burnett's vision of the "Beautiful Child" idealized young boys and girls as angelic, indeed flawless creatures, with no need for discipline or guidance by adults. Little Lord Fauntleroy, the American-born heir to an English dukedom, doesn't have to struggle to learn or to grow; instead, he has only to charm his gruff British grandfather in order to bring about a happy ending. In the same way, the little princess Sara Crew is a model of childlike virtue, and her only challenge is to endure hardship and ostracism without complaining.

With *The Secret Garden,* Burnett took up the mold of the "Beautiful Child" and smashed it into a thousand pieces. In earlier stories, Burnett's lavish descriptions of her child characters' beauty and adorable ways had inspired parents to leave their sons' curls uncut, dress them in velvet and lace, and encourage them to continue lisping in baby talk, just like Little Lord Fauntleroy. Now, on the first page of *The Secret Garden,* we find the heroine, Mary Lennox, described by Burnett as "the most disagreeable-looking child ever seen," with a "sour expression" and a disposition to match.

With *The Secret Garden,* Burnett shook off the trappings of the "Beautiful Child" and began to describe children whose challenge was not just to endure unpleasantness sweetly but actually to grow up and face the world. Mary Lennox isn't a child to coo over, but she seems real in a way the children of *Little Lord Fauntleroy* and *A Little Princess* never quite do. It's not surprising, then, that while we think of the two earlier stories as old-fashioned period pieces, *The Secret Garden* seems peculiarly modern and even personal. A friend recently made this distinction suddenly clear to me as we talked about children's stories and how they affect us. "I always thought of Sara Crewe as Shirley Temple," my friend remembered, "but Mary Lennox was me."

OF all classic children's books, *The Secret Garden* seems to make the greatest, most lasting impression. Those of us who read it in childhood remember *The Secret Garden* as a very special book about growing up. Perhaps it is because the magic kingdom of this story is so palpably real—an actual garden—that our memory of it remains vivid. And there is also the fact that the growth of Mary and Colin, expressed in the cultivation of the garden, is substantial and unequivocal. Their hearts come to flower in this magic kingdom, and open to give and receive love.

From the beginning of the story, Mary Lennox shows herself to be a compulsive gardener of sorts. In India, where she is indulged and kept out of the way by servants and ignored by her parents, we first see her as she sticks flowers into the earth, pretending to make a garden while inwardly seething. Her ayah is late in coming to her, and while thrusting hibiscus blossoms into heaps of dirt, she mutters the insults she plans to hurl when the servant finally does appear. She's the picture of a spoiled, miserable, destructive child, but there is also a part of her that senses even now the cure for her heart's sickness.

After Mary has been rescued by British troops and taken away from her home, where everyone else has died of cholera, she stays for a time with an English clergyman's family. Escaping from the children, whom she hates, she again pretends to make a little garden by herself. When Basil, one of the brothers in the family, offers her a friendly suggestion, Mary wheels on him and orders him away. Stung by her rejection, Basil mocks her with the all-too-appropriate nursery rhyme:

> Mistress Mary, quite contrary
> How does your garden grow?
> With silver bells, and cockle shells,
> And marigolds all in a row.

Your child sees that Mary's make-believe gardens, with their rootless flowers, are the result of her own anger and spite. Consequently, they don't accomplish anything worthwhile, and their harvest is only withered blossoms and more bitterness for Mary. She has the right idea—she can work to overcome the bad effects of her own indifferent upbringing by cultivating another kind of young life—but she lacks the proper materials, the right place, even the necessary energy and ambition to turn the imaginary into the real.

MARY finds what she needs in Yorkshire, at lonely Misselthwaite Manor, which seems at first an unlikely place for a child to thrive. Here Mary is left entirely on her own, with no ayah to dress her, no servants willing to play with her, and no toys or books to while away the cold northern days and evenings. Her uncle, Archibald Craven, is not there to greet her when she arrives; in fact, nothing and no one at Misselthwaite Manor is there expressly to please her, or to make her life easier, as they were in her home in India. She's even told to keep out of most of the rooms. Yet it is precisely this forbidding, cold atmosphere that sparks her into life and helps her to become a happy, growing child.

On the first morning, the Yorkshire servant, Martha, tells Mary to go out and play, suggesting that she walk around and look at the gardens on the estate. As she shows Mary out, Martha mentions that on Mr. Craven's orders, one of the gardens has been locked up and the key has been buried since the death of Mrs. Craven, the master's wife, ten years ago. Suddenly curious, Mary looks for the garden, and is disappointed when she can't find it.

She questions Ben Weatherstaff, the gardener, but he answers her gruffly. Then Mary sees a robin, a bird that Ben welcomes cheerily and calls in playful respect "th' head gardener." This robin represents nature itself, come to welcome Mary to her new home. The mere sight of the bird and Ben's cheerful greeting stir Mary's imagination, and suddenly she's talking to the robin as if it were a person.

When Mary, with surprising warmth, asks the robin to be her friend, he sings to her, and then flies away. In a way, Mary is asking nature for help, and the robin, it seems, understands this as if by magic, because he rewards Mary's first friendly gesture by telling her exactly what she needs to know. As Mary watches, the bird flies over the wall and into another garden—one, she realizes, that has no door. In return for Mary's offer of friendship, the robin has shown her the way to the secret garden.

MARY's improved health and temperament since she arrived in Yorkshire make it clear to your child that the earlier tantrums and disagreeable attitude were not an expression of Mary's true nature, but rather the result of the unwise manner in which she was raised. Like an untended garden, she'd been neglected, and allowed to wither and grow weedy. Now all that is beginning to change.

Mary is excited and curious about finding a way into the secret garden, but she has also begun to notice other interesting aspects of life at Misselthwaite, too. Very early she sees that Martha, though friendly, will not wait upon her or tolerate any tantrums. Although she's not accustomed to it, Mary begins to do things for herself and, to her surprise, discovers that she likes it. Instead of screaming at servants to obey her, as she did in India, Mary takes care of herself, and finds that freedom and independence are much more enjoyable than domination. She's on her way to being a child-hero rather than a tyrant.

The cooler weather of Yorkshire, the new activity, the walks through the gardens and on the moors on windy days, all combine to make Mary much brighter, more cheerful, and even prettier. The servants begin to notice that she is losing the pinched, yellowish cast in her face, and looking rosier and plumper. Her appetite increases, and she's eager to be out playing early in the morning rather than sulking.

But the greatest change that your child notices in Mary occurs on the inside. Life on the moors and in the large, mysterious house has "set her inactive brain to working" and even seems to be "awakening her imagination." She is curious about her surroundings—especially the secret garden—and about people, as well. Mary even wants to understand and speak the Yorkshire dialect she hears spoken by the servants—a kind of secret language that fascinates her awakening imagination.

LIKE Christopher Robin's Forest, Wonderland, and the River Bank, the secret garden has its own lessons to teach its child-ruler, and, through imagination, your own child. As always in the magic kingdom, the central values are growth and the acceptance of change.

While Mary is eagerly coming to enjoy the life around her—learning to jump rope, listening to servants talking, wondering about the secret garden—she finds to her delight that her new interest in the world is answered by a kind of magic in nature. The robin she made friends with the first morning, the one who showed her the way to the secret garden, calls to her from a flower bed where he's been digging for worms. When Mary comes closer, she finds that the robin has unearthed an old key. Now he calls to her again from the ivy-covered wall, and with the next gust of wind—

the same wind that put roses in Mary's cheeks—she sees what was concealed behind the ivy: a green door. The old key fits the lock, of course, and Mary opens the door to the secret garden itself, mysterious, neglected, and unseen for ten years.

Mary's first look at the inside of the secret garden, with its strangely beautiful tangles of vines and branches, surprises and intrigues her. Are the roses all dead, she wonders? Hoping that they are not, she walks carefully, as if the garden were actually asleep, and she marvels at the stillness within its walls, where no one has spoken for ten years.

Your child sees that the secret garden has already begun its magic, inspiring Mary first to curiosity, then to awe, and now to sympathy. She sees some tiny green shoots among the weeds—something is alive in here, after all—and it seems to her that the little plants can't breathe properly. Mary immediately begins to clear away the weeds and, when the green shoots have a bit more room, she feels better herself. She has identified with the garden through her imagination, and now she's ready to make some changes, so that both of them can grow.

Like your child, Mary has read about fairy-tale gardens where you might fall asleep for a hundred years, but this garden, she realizes, has been making her "wider awake every day" since she's heard of it. The secret garden at Misselthwaite Manor presents Mary with the real challenges of life—change, growth, learning—instead of offering escape from them, as fairy-tale gardens do.

THE challenges of the garden and Mary's eagerness to meet them make the secret garden a magic kingdom, a place Mary goes to prepare herself for growing up, so that she will be fully awake, and fully alive, to face the wider world. It is clear to your child that Mary sees the need for growth and change in the garden as soon as she enters it, because immediately she begins to pull the weeds that are choking the plants.

And Mary is intent on visiting the secret garden daily, to do the hard work that is needed to bring it back to life. She's eager to prune away all the dead foliage so the roses will bloom again, but she has no experience of real gardening. How can she get the help she needs without giving away the secret?

Exercising all her cleverness and care, Mary questions the gardener Ben Weatherstaff again, and manages this time to extract some information she can use to bring the garden back to life. But this indirect method doesn't work for long. For the secret garden to bloom again, Mary has to start pulling the weeds that are choking her own growth. It's not until she meets Martha's younger brother Dickon, and trusts him enough to share her secret, that Mary's work in the secret garden begins in earnest.

Dickon is a Yorkshire boy whose love of the moors and empathy with nature have taught him—it seems almost literally—about the secret life of plants and the languages of the birds. It is Dickon's knowledge of gardening that will make Mary's wish for the secret garden to bloom again a practical reality. Dickon's keen eyes can spot those rosebushes that are still "wick"—alive at the roots—and those that are dead and need to be hacked away. Dickon also knows which seeds should be planted in the flower beds, how to keep them growing, and where to weed.

Besides his gardening expertise, the twelve-year-old Dickon offers Mary her first friendship, freely and heartily. Mary, unaccustomed to accepting something without payment of some kind, at first thinks she must bargain for Dickon's help in the garden, but is at a loss about what to offer him. "If you will help me to make it alive I'll—I don't know what I'll do," she stammers. Dickon, who never expected any payment at all, happily misunderstands, and finishes the thought for her. "I'll tell thee what tha'll do," he says in his broad Yorkshire. "Tha'll get fat an' tha'll get as hungry as a young fox an' tha'll learn how to talk to th' robin same as I do. Eh! We'll have a lot o' fun."

Of course they'll have fun, but, as your child senses, this magic kingdom has a more serious purpose for Mary as well. "I've stolen a garden," Mary tells Dickon. "Nobody wants it, nobody cares for it, nobody ever goes into it. Perhaps everything is dead in it already; I don't know." Even before Dickon can respond, she bursts out passionately, "I don't care, I don't care! Nobody has any right to take it from me when I care about it and they don't. They're letting it die, all shut in by itself." When Dickon asks to see the garden, Mary leads him to the door and slowly opens it. "It's a secret garden," she says with some defiance, "and I'm the only one in the world who wants it to be alive."

ALREADY, Mary has changed greatly since she violently rebuffed a boy for daring to offer his help in her pretend garden. She finds herself able genuinely to like and to trust Dickon, and in sharing her secret with him she also makes clear the garden's meaning, expressing aloud for the first time why it is so important to her.

In speaking of the garden, Mary is speaking of herself, expressing the passionate resentment she feels for the way she's been raised, "all shut in" by herself, miserable and friendless, until, at ten, she's not even sure if anything inside her is living and able to grow. No one has offered her help in tending the garden within her, and, aware of her isolation for the first time in her life, she tells Dickon what she believes to be the sad truth: she is the only person in the world who wants the garden to live.

But in talking about her own loneliness in terms of the garden, Mary begins to put an end to her isolation. She finds a language to express what she needs, and a task that can serve as a bridge between herself and others. In reaching out to Dickon and asking for his help, Mary is admitting that she needs friendship as well as rebirth and growth, and Dickon happily responds.

As soon as he sees the garden, Dickon assures Mary that

there is plenty of life ready to blossom there, and that there will be "a fountain o' roses" in the spring if they both work to clear the way. Overjoyed, Mary promises to follow his directions carefully, and then, spontaneously, asks Dickon in his own Yorkshire dialect, "Does tha' like me?"

"That I does" is Dickon's pleased response. He also promises to keep the garden a secret, just as he keeps secret the nests and burrows of his animal friends. "Tha' art as safe as a missel thrush," Dickon tells Mary, when she reluctantly stops her work to go home.

In the house, Mary learns that she is to meet her uncle and guardian, Archibald Craven, for the first time. She's worried and a bit intimidated by what she has heard about her mysterious uncle, who, after ten years, is still mourning the death of his wife. Emboldened by her recent conversation with Dickon, she decides to speak up about her feelings and her needs, something that is still quite new for her. First she asks her uncle if she can be on her own for a while, without a nurse or a governess, and Mr. Craven agrees, mentioning that Mrs. Sowerby, Dickon and Martha's mother, had recommended a little freedom for Mary.

Then Mary blurts out her most important request. "Might I have a bit of earth?" she asks. "To plant seeds in—to make things grow—to see them come alive." Mr. Craven, after reflection, sees what a garden means to his strange little niece, and tells her, almost smiling for the first time, "When you see a bit of earth you want . . . take it, child, and make it come alive."

So Mary secures her garden without betraying its secret, and, since she has her uncle's permission, she doesn't have to think of it as "stolen" any longer. And this extraordinary development, something Mary—and your child as well— would have thought impossible an hour before, is the result of her secret conversation with Dickon in the garden.

Having confided her deepest feelings to a friend in this safe, magic place, she becomes better able to express herself publicly, and to a virtual stranger whom she's been anxious about meeting. Your child sees the magic at work already. The language of the secret garden frees Mary to take part in the language of the world, and to win a victory for her own growth.

After talking with her uncle, Mary runs back to the secret garden, hoping to share her exciting news with Dickon. When she arrives, though, Dickon is gone. Disappointed, Mary begins to wonder if Dickon were not a real boy at all, but just a wood fairy. Then she notices a sheet of paper with the message "I will cum bak," and a picture of a missel thrush in her nest. The secret garden partnership is sealed, then, with a promise of loyalty conveyed, appropriately, in a secret language.

YOUR own child is pleased to see that the secret garden hasn't turned Mary into an angel or a faultless Beautiful Child. Mary is the same person she's always been, strong-willed and inclined to be short-tempered at times. But now she is also able to see beyond herself, to enjoy other people, and to appreciate their friendship. In the terms of the secret garden, her true nature hasn't been uprooted, just weeded and cultivated, as it needed to be, for the sake of her own growth.

Before Mary can work in the secret garden with Dickon again, there are two full weeks of rain. This is a necessary part of the preparation for spring, Mary knows, and she's pleased with herself for taking the delay with an even temper instead of sulking or screaming as she might have in India. While she's confined to the house, she becomes keenly aware of the wild sound of the wind and rain outside, what the Yorkshire people call "wuthering." Mary, who is becoming more interested in people, imagines that it sounds "just like a person lost on the moor and wandering on and on crying." And it is through her imagination that she discovers the truth.

One night, as she lies awake listening to the wuthering, she suddenly hears crying coming from somewhere in the house. She gets out of bed and determines to follow the sound in order to find out who it is. She's heard crying like this in the house before, but she'd always been stopped or put off by the servants in her search for its source. Now, in the middle of the night, there is no one to interfere as Mary makes her way through the maze of corridors, listening all the while for the crying. Behind a tapestry she finds a door, and when she opens it she sees a boy her own age, lying awake in a big four-poster bed, crying, she can see, not so much from pain as from boredom and loneliness.

It's Colin, Mary's cousin, the ten-year-old son of Archibald Craven, who has been kept in his rooms and treated as an invalid all his life. His father, Colin tells Mary, "almost hates" him for being born at his mother's death, and for possibly inheriting from his father a malformation of the spine. Kept isolated from whatever life the strange house has to offer, Colin has been shut up and neglected, like the secret garden itself.

Not surprisingly, Colin has grown to be a fretful, angry, lonely, and frightened boy, and is developing a strong bent for hypochondria. Fresh air, he declares, would kill him. He doesn't consciously feign sickness, but he makes himself sick by becoming miserable and even hysterical with anxiety about the possibility of illness. The isolation combined with fear makes him a tyrant; screaming one moment, insisting that he's dying the next. His doctor and his father order all who care for Colin to pamper him constantly, no matter how eccentric or rude his behavior. Colin's moods, which terrify the servants, are his only way of participating in the daily life outside his bedroom door. That is, until his cousin Mary suddenly appears in his room.

COLIN's bad humor comes from an unhealthy upbringing— the same destructive combination of neglect and indulgence that Mary suffered in India. Although Mary isn't aware that she's been spoiled, she does see that Colin has been, and she observes with disgust that he thinks he can order anyone about, just like a young rajah she'd once seen in India.

Because Mary has become less likely to be annoyed by people, she can talk with her cousin and draw him out a bit, something new for both of them. When by accident Mary mentions the secret garden, Colin seizes on it as eagerly as Mary did when she first arrived at Misselthwaite and was as bored and lonely as Colin. But since Colin is confined to his room and unable to ramble around the grounds on his own to look for the secret garden as Mary did, he announces, like a young rajah, that he'll enter this magical place the wrong way—by force of will. "I want to see that garden," he tells Mary imperiously. "I am going to make them open the door."

Mary is panicked by Colin's idea to force his way into the garden. In a flash, the effect of her casual words comes home to her—she's told the secret, she'll never be able to see Dickon anymore and weed and plant in peace, safe as a missel thrush in her nest. Now this boy will open the garden door to everyone, and it won't be a secret garden full of magic anymore, just a regular garden that needs some pruning. Her only chance to save her magic kingdom is to somehow make Colin see it as she did the first time, as an enchanted place, magically revealed to her by a robin and the wind.

For the moment, Mary keeps to herself the fact that she has already been inside the garden. She promises that if Colin keeps the secret, she will find the key and the door, and a boy to push his chair, and that they will all keep the secret together as they watch the garden come to life again. Then Mary describes what the garden might look like, with roses and birds' nests, and a robin hopping and talking to them in his own funny way. Pleased with the picture Mary paints for him, and assuming that she's imagining all this, Colin agrees to keep the secret. He hopes, someday, to enter this magic, secret place on its own terms. "I should not mind fresh air in a secret garden," he decides.

After telling him the story of the garden, Mary prepares to leave. But before she goes, she helps her restless and over-tired cousin to fall asleep. Stroking his hand gently, she softly sings a song in Hindustani, as her ayah used to do for her. It works wonderfully, this secret language of childhood, and Mary is able to leave the room quietly, having found another friend and partner for the secret garden.

JUST as the conversation in the secret garden prepares and strengthens Mary for speaking up to her uncle, her friendship with Dickon enables her to befriend her cousin. Because of the changes brought about by Dickon and the secret garden, Mary is able to listen to the ill-tempered Colin, sympathize with him, and help him to change the situation he finds so hopeless and miserable.

So when she befriends Colin and helps him to see the world beyond his lonely sickroom, she isn't a ministering angel. Instead, in the words of Colin's long-suffering nurse, sometimes she can be "a vixen of a sister to fight with," the kind of companion the boy has needed all along.

When Colin, in self-pity, confides miserably to Mary that he thinks everyone in the house wishes he would die, Mary snaps back that he should will himself to live, just to spite them. And when the boy throws one of his tyrannical temper tantrums because his cousin has gone outside one sunny day, Mary shocks him into silence with her own show of temper, shouting back at him, flouting his threats, and declaring furiously, "I wish everybody would run out of the house and let you scream yourself to death!"

Mary gives Colin the benefit of her resistance, playing for him the part of the wind on the moor that put roses in her own cheeks. But after Colin's tantrum is over, Mary confides to him that she's found the door into the secret garden. She promises to bring him there, and then lulls him to sleep with a vision of the secret garden, every day growing greener, waiting for him.

LIKE the robin, Mary leads Colin gradually to the wall of the secret garden, and will show him the way when the time is right. By this point in the story, your child sympathizes with Colin as much as Mary does, and, like Mary, wants to see him put aside the airs of a young sickly rajah and accept the challenges of the magic kingdom that await him in the secret garden.

When Mary first tells Colin about her friend Dickon, she explains that Dickon seems to be able to charm the moor animals just as the native Indians charm snakes. Colin is fascinated and, although he doesn't like to be stared at and has even bitten a condescending stranger who came too close to him, he mentions to Mary that he wouldn't mind being looked at by Dickon. "He is an animal charmer," Colin reasons, "and I am a boy animal."

This is the first unself-conscious truth Colin admits about himself, and the quaintness of its expression makes both Mary and Colin laugh. Laughter, Dickon's mother says, can fend off the worst sickness, and this natural medicine works on the sickly Colin, making him stronger day by day.

Laughter brings him out of his morose, hypersensitive moodiness, and actually begins to dispel his fear of dying. Dickon, hearing Mary speak in Yorkshire dialect in admiring imitation of him, encourages her to "talk a bit o' Yorkshire" to Colin to make him laugh. It works, and the good humor and curiosity Colin feels upon hearing the dialect inspires the boy to tell his cousin he'd like to hear and see Dickon for himself.

When Mary hears this, she is suddenly convinced that Colin is ready to share the entire truth about the secret garden. She tells him that she's already been inside, that she and Dickon have been going there for weeks, but that she was not sure until now that she could safely tell him about it. One day soon, Mary promises, all three of them will enter the garden together.

It has been years since the young master left the house, and the doctor and servants need some convincing before Colin is permitted to be outside for a time. The day that Colin, Mary, and Dickon plan to go to the secret garden together, Colin orders the gardeners to stay away from the Long Walk, where the entrance to the garden is, so that no one will see where the friends are going.

That afternoon, Dickon pushes Colin's chair down the path while Mary points out the place she first saw the robin, then the clump of earth that concealed the key, and finally the door behind the green curtain of ivy. Before he knows it, Colin is inside the secret garden itself, the place he has dreamed of and longed for ever since the first night Mary followed the sound of his crying to the lonely sickroom. Overjoyed, he cries, "I shall get well! And I shall live forever and ever and ever!"

By this time, spring has come to Yorkshire, and all of Mary and Dickon's work is beginning to make the secret garden come alive again. Colin looks around in amazement at the flowering trees, budding plants, and the vines on the garden walls, slowly changing from gray to green. Dickon pushes Colin's chair up and down the paths within the secret garden, and it seems that he is being "taken in state round the country of a magic king and queen and shown all the mysterious riches it contained."

Apart from the rest of the world, a place where children rule and growth is a heroic challenge, the secret garden is the ultimate magic kingdom, and Colin senses immediately its purpose and value. "I'm going to see everything grow here," he declares happily. "I'm going to grow here myself."

COLIN's inability to stand and walk doesn't have a physical cause, but comes from being treated like an invalid rather than an ordinary child. No one has expected him to walk for years, and so, of course, he can't. And, psychologically, he's never had the experience of being independent, making his own decisions and then carrying them out himself. Literally, he's never had to stand up for himself and defend his rights. But an afternoon in the secret garden will change that.

Peering over the wall, Ben Weatherstaff, the gruff gardener Mary met shortly after her arrival, suddenly sees three children in the garden he believes to be locked. Recognizing Mary, he shakes his fist at her and scolds her roundly for entering the forbidden place. Outraged by this treatment of his cousin, Colin shouts to Dickon to wheel him over to the wall, right in front of Ben Weatherstaff.

This is a challenge that strikes at the heart, and Colin is going to assert his will not by hysterics or tantrums, but by a simple, passionate declaration of truth. He has every right to be here with his cousin and their friend. This garden is, after all, part of Colin's home. He has also been told that it was a place his mother especially loved. Moreover, he *wants* to be here, feeling sure that this garden is somehow, magically, connected to his own growth, and even his chances for life.

Before he'd heard about the secret garden, Colin believed himself a hopeless invalid, likely to die soon and unable to do anything to prevent it. Since then, he's felt stronger day by day, found a cousin, and made a friend. And now he's even out in the fresh air, unafraid and enjoying himself for the first time in his life.

All of this has happened because of Colin's imaginative connection with the secret garden, the magic link created and nurtured by Mary, who was herself transformed by the garden. Now that his dream has finally become a reality, and he is actually in the secret garden himself, Colin is prepared to defend his chances for a happier life. From his chair, he boldly challenges the gardener with a curt, "Do you know who I am?"

Ben Weatherstaff has never seen Colin, although he immediately sees the boy's resemblance to his mother. But Ben, like many of the other servants, has come to believe that Colin is physically deformed. Surprised by Colin's sudden appearance and taken aback by his bold challenge, Ben tactlessly blurts out what he's thinking: "Tha' hasn't got a crooked back? . . . tha' hasn't got crooked legs?"

Colin, angry and insulted, is suddenly "filled with a power

he had never known before, an almost unnatural strength."
He throws the lap rugs to the ground and suddenly stands
upright in front of the wheelchair, with the defiant cry,
"Look at me! . . . Just look at me—you! Just look at me!"

It is a moment of supreme self-assertion, a realization of his
power that changes Colin in his own eyes, and in everyone
else's, forever. Calling him "young Mester," Ben Weatherstaff now pays royal homage to Colin by arranging for him
to plant his own rose there in the secret garden, "same as th'
king does when he goes to a new place." Standing up for
himself, then, claiming his birthright and his dignity, Colin
becomes the master of the secret garden, ruler of the magic
kingdom.

WITH Mary and Dickon, your child shares imaginatively in
Colin's triumph, and in the laughter among the children that
ends their extraordinary day. Like a secret language, that
laughter is a sign of their shared imagination and love for one
another, as well as a spontaneous expression of the bond
created by the magic of the secret garden.

The Yorkshire dialect that Dickon speaks and Colin and
Mary adopt in the garden seems another secret language of
love and imagination, suited to the beauty and mystery of the
changes in nature as well as the changes they're going through
themselves. And as Colin gradually builds his strength in the
secret garden, Mary finds that she can actually help him to
walk by chanting under her breath, "You can do it! You can
do it!"

This prompts Colin to conduct what he proudly calls "experiments" in his own growth, and leads him to generalize
that if the secret language of love and encouragement can
have a good effect on his physical recovery, it may work
other changes as well. The children call this mysterious helping power "Magic," and surmise that its influence may extend even beyond the garden walls. You and your own child
know already that it's the same magic you've heard together
on the wind in the willows.

* * *

BEFORE the children in the secret garden have proof of their theory, your own child sees the direct effect of the Magic on Colin's father, who is traveling aimlessly through Europe, after ten years still unreconciled to his wife's death and his son's life. Colin has planned to surprise his father with his sudden recovery and, in healing himself, to heal the breach that divides father and son. But the garden's Magic is already at work on Archibald Craven, although Colin, Mary, and Dickon aren't aware of it.

Far away, in the Austrian mountains, the lonely man rests by a stream, and suddenly the sound of the running water seems to him like laughter. Astounded by the change he feels, the melting away of his sad thoughts, he says he feels "as if—I were alive!" This inspiration comes to him on the day Colin enters the garden and cries, "I am going to live forever and ever and ever!" Without knowing it, Archibald Craven is "coming alive with the garden," just as Mary and Colin are. The children's laughter and Colin's shout of joy have reached him magically.

A few days later, Colin's father has a dream that his wife is calling him to come to her "in the garden" she loved so much, the one he locked up after her death. He is intrigued by the strange dream, and when he receives a letter from Dickon's mother encouraging him to come home, because "I think your lady would ask you to come if she was here," he immediately starts back to Misselthwaite. When he arrives, the housekeeper tells him that Colin has changed much since he left, and is now "in the garden."

With that magical phrase echoing in his mind, the father is drawn as if in a dream toward the rose garden he had thought abandoned and neglected. Now he hears children's laughter as he comes near the ivy-covered wall. Suddenly the door opens and a tall, handsome boy runs out and nearly into his arms, without seeing him.

It's Colin. Amazed, the father follows his son into the garden, where he hears the whole story of Colin's recovery and the magic of the secret garden. Then, laughing, they walk out of the garden together and back to the house, where all the servants stare in astonishment at the father and son, joyful and healthy, a happy family at last.

YOUR child has watched the almost miraculous changes in Colin and in Mary—nothing less than an abundance of health and happiness—brought about by the ineffable magic of certain words and a special place, a secret language in a secret garden. Like Mowgli, Colin enters the secret garden weak and vulnerable, but walks out of it strong and proud, all grown up. And like Mowgli, who grants the Favor of the Jungle to his younger brother, Mary finds that part of the joy of the magic she has discovered lies in passing it on to her cousin and creating more magic.

Whether set in a Yorkshire garden or the jungles of India, the story of the magic kingdom is the same. A child finds a secret door to a magic place, apart from ordinary life. Here he faces challenges that will show his true nature and make him the triumphant ruler of the magic kingdom. And your own child goes through it all in imagination, facing down absurdity and acting decisively, discovering courage and intelligence, strength of character and nobility of purpose.

Of course, the reason for entering the secret garden as a child is to be able someday to leave it a grown-up, but there is a part of us that is somehow still connected to it, mysteriously, magically. A phrase, a scent, and suddenly we're in the garden again, children once more.

A friend, born on the Indian subcontinent and educated in British schools there, was recently telling me about a typical afternoon in his childhood in what was then East Bengal. When school let out for the day he was free, and while his mother, a teacher at the school, remained behind to prepare for the next day's lessons, my friend liked to walk across the street to the library of the British Embassy and browse contentedly in the stacks for an hour or so.

As he was describing this high point of his daily routine when he was a child, he suddenly stopped, a bit overwhelmed by memory. Smiling, he remarked with some surprise that he could still see the reading room and his favorite books, feel the texture of their bindings, and sense the pleasant coolness and even the wonderful fragrance of the library, though he hadn't been there for over twenty-five years.

For all of us who grew up being read to and then reading on our own, the library was, and always will be, a kind of secret garden, a place of quiet and solitude as well as adventure and friendship and growth. As children, with a book in the library or at home in a favorite spot, we were alone and yet in company with everyone who had read the book before us and who would read it after us.

Most of all, we were with each hero—Alice, Christopher Robin, Mole, Mary, Mowgli—identifying in imagination, and sharing the challenges and triumphs of the magic kingdom. And so it will be with your child.

CHAPTER FIVE

Flights of Imagination

IT is when your child is reading, imaginatively immersed in a book, that he is closest to creating his own self in reality. In the very private act of reading, your child discovers a landscape of childhood that belongs to all of us; a landscape that gives shape and meaning not only to our common sense of culture, but to your own child's growing sense of himself.

We talk about growing up as "spreading your wings and flying," and we mean it to describe finding your own sense of balance and power, apart from anyone or anything else. It is a wonderfully thrilling image, the epitome of freedom, full of the sense of being entirely in control and, literally, above it all.

The first experience your child has of soaring by himself at will is the flight of imagination through the pages of a book. Fluency in reading sets your child free to move through the story on his own, gliding over its length as he chooses, while seeing the whole from a new and higher perspective.

And many of the stories your child will read offer the fantasy of flying through the power of the magic kingdom. Alice flies briefly and unexpectedly in the Looking-Glass World, and Dorothy Gale arrives in Oz by way of a cyclone. When Toad takes a sudden flight after crashing the car he's been driving, he glories in freedom and grace, hoping to turn into a "Toadbird" before landing with a flop in the meadow.

The best kind of flying, though, isn't just an end in itself. Instead, it's part of an even bigger adventure that opens a new world. Whenever it happens in the magic kingdom, it signals the beginning of a journey through imagination that will lead at last to the path of wisdom. Flying is a magic gift that comes unexpectedly, but at just the right time, to help in the difficult and crucial passage between childhood and adolescence.

* * *

OF course, when we think of classic children's stories that feature flying, the first that spring to mind are *Peter Pan,* by J. M. Barrie, and *Mary Poppins,* by P. L. Travers. Both stories have enjoyed enduring popularity, in their original forms and as adaptations in films, animation, and stage productions. No one tires, it seems, of a story about children living an ordinary life until they suddenly meet someone extraordinary who unexpectedly opens up a magic kingdom, a world of imagination, where anything is possible.

At first, the characters Peter Pan and Mary Poppins seem to be almost opposites. After all, Peter is a mischievous boy and Mary is a grown-up nanny. Peter loves chaos and Mary insists on order. Peter takes Wendy, Michael, and John to his own Neverland, while Mary comes to stay with the Banks children in their London house. But despite their differences, Peter and Mary bring the same gift to the nurseries in which they suddenly, magically, take charge. In winning the trust of their child-friends, Peter and Mary teach them to trust themselves, and when this happens, the children can fly.

THE first time Mary Poppins takes Jane and Michael on an outing, to her Uncle Albert's for tea, she melts their polite, shy reserve with her own magical method. By accident—or is it?—she has brought the children there on a day that her uncle spends merrily floating around the ceiling. His laughter buoys him up, Uncle Albert breathlessly explains, whenever his birthday falls on a Friday.

Before her uncle, Mary Poppins is solemn and grim, and while she lectures him on his behavior, Jane and Michael stand beside her in confusion, trying to remain quiet and polite, as they feel they must under such strange circumstances. But as Uncle Albert continues to bob hilariously around the ceiling, the children just can't keep straight faces any longer. They burst into giggles—their natural, spontaneous response to the ridiculous situation—and immediately rise in the air themselves, flying up to meet Mary's delighted uncle for a tea party on the ceiling. With a show of disapproval, Mary joins them there, making it clear as she does so that she can fly whenever she wants to, laughing or not.

It is typical of Mary Poppins that she doesn't teach the children or coax them into flying, as if it were something they needed to learn or be talked into. Instead, she creates a situation in which simply yielding to their true feelings will lift the children up off the ground. If she wanted, of course, Mary could make Jane and Michael fly, just as she lifts the tea-table and the landlady up to the ceiling for her convenience. But that would prove only *her* power, not the children's. Mary's aim, in this outing and in the many that follow, is not to make the children dependent on her for magic, but to reveal to Jane and Michael the magic that lies within *them*.

MARY Poppins sees the potential in the children she cares for because of her privileged knowledge of childhood. When babies are born, Mary knows, they can talk and understand perfectly, and even speak with the birds. It's only grown-ups who don't speak the common language of living things.

But when babies' teeth come in, they forget the wonders they can do. Still, every child has the ability to learn and to live imaginatively as part of nature, beyond the restraints of conventional city life. It's simply a matter of awakening the memories inside.

Special times and places help in rousing the true self within children, and Mary Poppins takes these opportunities to teach Jane and Michael to understand the magic within them. And so the children find themselves visiting the zoo for Mary Poppins's birthday at the full moon, precisely the right time for such magic. Everything's upside-down, it seems, with all the cages open, and people offering animals rides.

This visit to the zoo outdoes even a tea party on the ceiling for unconventionality, and at the center of the celebration is Mary Poppins herself. She presides over the topsy-turvy zoo, like a child in a magic kingdom, and she calls for Jane and Michael to join her. That night, they are initiated into a mystery—or reminded of it—through the power of Mary's birthday and the full moon.

All the animals are dancing around, when suddenly the children hear a voice—just as Mole and Ratty hear the wind in the willows—and it sings of unity. Bird, beast, star, child—all are one, the voice intones; all share the same life, the same power. It is something we all knew before cutting our first teeth, but it takes Mary Poppins, in her own special way, to remind us.

AN important part of Mary Poppins's great appeal for children comes from her insistence on doing things her own way. From her unexpected arrival at the Bankses' house, when, unobserved except by Jane and Michael, she slides up the bannister, Mary seems, by some magic, to have managed to take on the appearance of an adult while remaining a child.

Self-willed and unpredictable, Mary is not the kind of adult who smothers a child with affection and sympathy. Instead, she gives her charges the benefit of her assertive, independent example, and it frees them, the same way the blustery moor wind enlivens Mary Lennox and awakens her imagination.

And Mary Poppins, like Mary Lennox, plays the part of "a vixen of a sister to fight with" rather than a nursery angel, to the surprise of Jane and Michael. Her boldness, her tricks, even her egotism—she pronounces herself to be practically perfect—work like a dare, a challenge to the quiet children to go out into the world and to try more, explore more, as she does, and, inevitably, to spread their wings and fly.

TRAVERS saves for last the image of Mary Poppins we most treasure—the carefully dressed governess with a carpetbag in one hand, open umbrella in the other, flying over the housetops. The combination of primness and magic, Mary Poppins's unique style, comes across unforgettably as the inspired balancing of the carpetbag and umbrella—two ordinary objects—suddenly becomes extraordinary in her hands.

This image of Mary Poppins, so much a part of popular culture, is captured in a lean and unsentimental pen-and-ink drawing by Mary Shepard, the daughter of E. H. Shepard, illustrator of the *Pooh* books and *The Wind in the Willows*. In all her illustrations for *Mary Poppins*, she shows us a wiry and lithe rather than cuddly nanny, with a look that is not so much endearing as invigorating. True to the story, Shepard gives life and dimension to the animated spirit of Mary Poppins and her ability to motivate and enliven the children she cares for through her imaginative power and her will.

Having promised to stay with the Banks children until the wind changes, Mary departs on it, typically, in her own way. As she does, Jane and Michael watch her in wonder from the window of the nursery that their extraordinary nanny has transformed into a magic kingdom, a place where they have become aware of the power that was hidden within themselves.

IN *Peter Pan,* your child finds another London nursery invaded without warning by a magic character who flies and who dares quiet, obedient children to follow. Peter Pan, like Mary Poppins, is not above using trickery to get his way, and entrances children not by sweetness or kindness, but by a kind of exhilarating egotism.

Many stories attest to our need for fantasy, but *Peter Pan* is a story that introduces the idea that fantasy needs all of us, too, and that our belief in an imaginary world is literally vital to it. The magic of this relationship, which lies at the heart of *Peter Pan* and has made the story popular and beloved for generations, finds expression in a single, memorable question.

"Do you believe in fairies?" Peter Pan entreated the first-night audience of Barrie's play, as a last desperate attempt to

[131]

save Tinker Bell's life. "If you believe, wave your pocket-handkerchiefs and clap your hands!" No one could predict how *Peter Pan* would be received that night, and the celebrated actress Nina Boucicault, as Peter, dreaded the moment when she would have to ask the audience to save the fairy Tinker Bell with their applause. Concerned himself, Barrie arranged at the last moment for the orchestra to applaud if the audience didn't, but if it took that emergency measure to save Tink, it would certainly be the death of *Peter Pan*.

Barrie's precaution was unnecessary. From that premiere performance, on the evening of December 27, 1904, at London's Duke of York's Theatre, audiences have applauded and cheered, their expression of belief giving life to the fairy Tinker Bell, and to Barrie's creation as a whole.

The audience at the opening of *Peter Pan,* with few, if any, children among them, had arrived that night expecting another typically witty, sophisticated drama of modern relationships from the successful playwright Barrie. Instead, the curtain rose to reveal a nursery, where a Newfoundland dog was busily getting a little boy ready for his bath. Later, nearly all the principal characters were flying on stage, and a little, darting beam of light was addressed all night as "Tinker Bell," apparently a character, too.

Unlike his other plays, *Peter Pan* had come from the part of Barrie's adult life that he most relished—his friendship with the five boys of the Llewelyn-Davies family. The idea for Neverland, and for Peter Pan himself, arose from the imaginative play Barrie and the boys enjoyed together as they pretended to be shipwrecked, battled pirates, and rescued one another. Barrie was a fine amateur photographer, as Charles Dodgson was, and he took pictures of the brothers at play. How he thought of producing a play from their collaborative fantasy, Barrie claimed he didn't remember, but the boys were thoroughly delighted when *Peter Pan* was enthusiastically received in both London and New York. It was as if their own Peter Pan had suddenly become real enough to be everyone's hero, and had conquered the world.

Peter Pan was, and still is, a perennial stage classic, repeated in London every Christmas. By 1911, Barrie had written the story as a book, originally titled *Peter and Wendy,* and suddenly Neverland became a year-round excursion of imagination. The excitement that children and their parents had enjoyed in the theatre could be experienced at home, too.

Now, whenever he's wanted, Peter Pan can be conjured up by the simple opening of a book. Your child's room becomes the Darlings' nursery, and Peter himself will appear at the window to show the way to Neverland, the magic kingdom each child has all for her own, even while sharing it with the world.

BEFORE Peter Pan arrives, your child gets a wonderful and comically ironic introduction to the Darling family. The narrator presents Father Darling as the model parent, but then undercuts that impression immediately by showing his behavior and assumptions about what he thinks is important.

Of course, Mother Darling's most characteristic thoughts revolve around the children, Wendy, John, and Michael, but Father Darling is concerned about money and what the neighbors think of him. Father Darling especially is prey to financial and social anxieties, and he feverishly calculates the expense of having children while maintaining the dignity of his proper position, presiding over something called "stocks and shares." Barrie's tone here makes clear to your child how misguided and funny—how different from *you*—some parents can be.

Both Mother and Father Darling's concerns find a center in the children's nanny and her place in their home. With only limited means, yet eager to provide for their own family what the neighbors have for theirs, the Darlings hire Nana, a Newfoundland dog, to care for the children. Nana is a treasure, Mother insists, and very responsible, but Father can't help thinking that the neighbors must think less of him—that even Nana must think less of him—for engaging a dog as a nanny and for letting her run the nursery in her own way.

Nana has been a source of embarrassment for Father for some time, and one evening these unresolved misgivings about who is in charge explode in a battle of wills, and Nana is sent outside to be chained up. Father is now absolutely certain that everything is under control in the nursery, but he has unwittingly left the way clear for Peter Pan to enter.

PETER has been in the habit of coming to the Darlings' nursery window unobserved, with the fairy Tinker Bell, to hear the stories Mother tells. The last time he came, he had to leave so quickly when discovered by the vigilant Nana that he left his shadow behind.

When Wendy awakens during the night that Nana is chained in the yard, she sees Peter sitting on the floor, trying to stick his shadow on with soap. Unafraid and wanting to help, Wendy sews the shadow back on, and during their polite conversation turns up some fascinating details about Peter's life. He ran away as a baby; now he refuses to grow up, lives in Neverland with the Lost Boys, understands the language of the fairies, and can fly.

When Peter learns that Wendy knows lots of stories and enjoys taking care of boys, he asks her to fly with him to Neverland to tell stories and to be a mother to his Lost Boys. At first Wendy refuses—she can't fly, and anyway she mustn't leave home—but Peter's tempting descriptions of the mermaids in Neverland, the fun of flying, and the happy times she'll have playing mother to the Lost Boys have their effect. Wendy wakes her brothers and all three prepare themselves to learn to fly.

But flying, like all magic, has its own rules. It can't be approached deliberately or consciously. It has to come as a surprise, or be seen as misbehavior, and the teacher should only grudgingly approve, only partially cooperate.

Eager to learn, Wendy, Michael, and John pay strict attention to Peter's instructions and try their best to imitate him, but with no success. Peter tells them to think lovely thoughts, and they do, but when they climb on their beds and jump, they go down to the floor instead of up in the air.

Finally, Peter, who has been teasing the children by being only partially honest, blows fairy dust on them. With wonderful thoughts and the fairy dust, Wendy and her brothers rise in the air immediately, and find to their delight that they can fly. A few times around the room, and John suggests they try flying outside, into the night. This is what Peter has been waiting for, and boldly he leads them out of the nursery window, away to Neverland, with the stars to show the way: "second to the right, and straight on till morning."

so the Darling children fly out their nursery window with Peter to Neverland, a magic kingdom they have each imagined in their own minds. In our dreams, Barrie explains, we each find our own Neverland, but Wendy, John, and Michael are about to experience fantasy in a different way. The Neverland we all share, the landscape of childhood imagination itself, has been looking for the Darling children, and when it finds them, they will be drawn to that "nicely crammed" island of adventure and magically invited in, just as Mary Lennox is summoned to the secret garden. For despite all its variety, we discover, Neverland is incomplete without the Darling children, especially Wendy, whom Peter has brought to be its pretend-mother.

Mrs. Darling, the children's real mother, thinks of the world of London and the world of Neverland as two different, completely separate domains, divided always by a curtain or a film. When she suddenly awakens one night and sees Peter in the nursery, she's alarmed that Neverland has somehow come so close to the real world. She's shocked that a boy has actually stepped through what should be an impassable barrier. Her grown-up belief that reality and fantasy are two entirely separate things drives Peter away, but his shadow remains, the proof that Mrs. Darling's views don't conform to the facts.

The night Peter comes to retrieve his shadow and take the Darling children back with him to Neverland, he introduces a new idea about the borders of fantasy and reality. The fantasy of Neverland and the reality of London, Peter explains, aren't entirely separate. Once Peter lived in London, and so did the Lost Boys, and though they're at home in Neverland now, they still need part of the real world—stories told in London—to make them all happy.

And reality has a crucial effect on fantasy. Although children can't fly without fairy dust, the fairies themselves are born with a human baby's first laugh, and every time a child stops believing in fairies, one of them dies. And if we doubt this, Barrie makes his point in what is perhaps the most memorable part of the story, when your own child is called upon to prove the power she holds over Neverland. The fairy Tinker Bell, you remember, has drunk the poison intended for Peter, and is now dying. As her light fades, she whispers that she might get well if children believed in fairies. When Peter asks all the children who are close by Neverland to clap their hands, Tinker Bell sits up attentively and listens to hear whether she will live. And Barrie has placed that decision, literally, in your child's hands.

FOR Wendy, and for your own child, Peter Pan's "nicely crammed" Neverland is more than just a place for make-believe fun. It's also a magic kingdom, and, like every magic kingdom, it presents the challenge to grow. On the verge of growing up herself, Wendy meets the boy who won't grow up. Together they create a magic bond between fantasy and reality that enables Wendy to preserve her childlike imagination through adolescence and into adulthood, when she can pass along her Neverland adventure like a gift to her own child.

Neverland is a place where this bond can be made, for, like Christopher Robin's Forest, reality in Neverland can be molded and shaped by the power of symbols and gestures, words and imagination. In the Forest, Christopher Robin can smooth out problems among his friends simply with talk, a suggestion, even with laughter. In Neverland, reality is equally adaptable, and Wendy must rely on its flexibility even before she has set foot on the island.

Flying over the Lost Boys' home, lost herself and betrayed by the jealous Tinker Bell, Wendy is shot by Tootles's arrow and falls to earth, apparently dead. When Peter arrives and Tinker Bell's treachery is revealed, it is also discovered that the arrow was stopped by a button Wendy is wearing on a chain around her neck, a gift Peter believes to be his kiss. With a gesture of affection—even though it's a bit confused— Wendy's life has been saved, and in turn she saves Tinker Bell and Tootles from punishment with another gesture—her upraised arm stays Peter's hand.

Wendy is still unable to sit or stand up, so a "doctor" pretends to cure her. The promise of a house-building revives Wendy enough for her to be able to dream aloud her instructions for an ideal cottage. Peter, her brothers, and the Lost Boys construct a house around Wendy while she sleeps, and when it is complete she suddenly appears at the door, come back to life as mother of the boys, ready to enter Neverland's endless fantasy play.

EVERYDAY life in Neverland consists of the playing out in reality of familiar fantasies. In fact, the first real glimpse we get of Neverland attests to this endless collaborative game of make-believe. From above the island, we can see Captain Hook and the pirates skulking after the Lost Boys, Tiger Lily and her tribe hunting the pirates, and the wild beasts tracking the tribe, all circling around and around without stopping. For Peter and his boys, make-believe inevitably involves battles, chases, and escapes.

But however real the danger feels at times, no reality can withstand the power of a child's command, in word or gesture. If the wolves approach the Lost Boys, ready to attack, the animals can be put to rout when the boys all look at them through their legs. If the pirates tie the princess Tiger Lily to a rock so she will drown in the rising tide at Mermaids' Lagoon, Peter can free her by giving the order in Captain Hook's voice. Even when an encounter with the terrible Hook leaves Peter himself wounded and stranded on the rock, with the tide rising fast, a heroic gesture, his cry "To die will be an awfully big adventure," is enough to make certain his rescue.

WENDY chooses to take little or no part in the battling kind of imaginative play, even though she is sometimes drawn into it despite herself. Instead, because she's an older child, Wendy's make-believe play looks forward to adulthood, and her favorite fantasy is a vision of the reality that awaits her on the other side of adolescence.

So, after Peter and the boys spend the day in the forest, they return to their underground home, where Wendy is in charge. Here, as the pretend-mother, she fusses, soothes, encourages, and disciplines her "children," with Peter—another older child—as a sort of unofficial father.

But Wendy's most important task, the challenge she has come to this magic kingdom in order to face, is keeping a sense of reality always nearby, as a sort of night-light or counterbalance to the fantasy life of Neverland. Before bedtime, Wendy, like all mothers, tells a story to her children. In the Darling children's London home, the stories told had been of Neverland, the world of fantasy, so in Neverland the stories are of London, the world of reality.

The purpose of the stories is to keep the reality of the London world alive in her brothers' memory and to reintroduce it to the Lost Boys, for the sake of the children's balance and the good of both worlds. The happy ending of Wendy's bedtime story is the welcoming open window of the nursery and the promise that a mother always waits patiently within, whenever the children decide to leave make-believe and return to ordinary life.

As long as she is able to maintain the imaginative link between fantasy and reality, Wendy is happy and makes her play family happy, too. But one evening, the collaborative fantasy of parenthood that she enjoys with Peter breaks down. Peter asks Wendy to assure him that he isn't *really* grown-up, as they are pretending to be. When she does so, Peter is relieved, but Wendy is a little disappointed. Her happy mood broken, she asks Peter in turn for a little reassurance. What are his feelings for her? Peter replies instantly, "Those of a devoted son, Wendy."

It's as if, in the middle of the game of jump rope, Peter had simply dropped his end and walked away. He has switched roles and retreated from the collaboration of the two oldest children, because, unlike Wendy, he doesn't want to imagine being grown-up. He *won't* grow up.

BUT the real break between Peter and Wendy is still to come. As Wendy concludes her ritual bedtime story about the children who flew away to Neverland and then returned to their London nursery to find the window still open, their mother waiting, Peter delivers a dark pronouncement. Wendy is wrong about mothers, he insists. They don't wait patiently for your return. If you're gone long enough, your mother will forget you. *He* flew back once, he tells Wendy and the boys, but the window was shut and barred, and when he peeked in the room, he found another little boy in his bed.

In saying this, Peter takes complete control of both the fantasy and the reality that Wendy has been nurturing for the time she has been a pretend-mother. All this time, Wendy has been using her imagination as a bridge to lead to the world outside Neverland—her grown-up future, the Darlings' home in London—but Peter has now destroyed this vital link with his story.

In Neverland, the land where any adventure you can imagine can be lived out, the children suddenly can't believe in the return to London without fearing that it may not be possible. Instead of turning their interest away from London and back toward him, as Peter had anticipated, his story has the opposite effect. The children panic. They must fly home now—maybe it's not too late, and the window may still be open, their mother waiting.

WHEN Peter and Wendy's collaborative make-believe breaks apart, they part, too, Peter going to sulk alone and Wendy to pack up and leave immediately, with her brothers and the Lost Boys, for London. And as soon as Peter and Wendy go their separate ways, serious danger befalls them both. Wendy and the boys are kidnapped by the pirates, and Peter's medicine is poisoned by Hook. It's as if the pirates had been waiting on purpose for the alliance between Wendy and Peter—and the bond between fantasy and reality—to break and leave both vulnerable. Now that it has happened, the pirates make their move.

To prove to himself that he's not troubled or sorry about Wendy's departure, Peter decides to laugh rather than cry himself to sleep. And it is when he's asleep, the traces of laughter still evident in his features, that Hook creeps into Peter's underground home to destroy him.

When Hook sees that Peter is sleeping, he almost yields to an instinct to leave him alone and undisturbed. But the laughter in Peter's expression irritates Hook so much that he poisons Peter's medicine—Peter hasn't taken it, to spite Wendy further—and then leaves to join the pirates and the captives on board the ship.

As Hook runs through the forest, bragging of the night's evil deeds, Tinker Bell hears him and flies to wake Peter. She tells him that Wendy and the boys have been taken prisoner by the pirates, and Peter at once jumps to his feet to rescue them. Then, as he reaches for his dagger, Peter suddenly regrets his display of indifference and, wishing somehow to make up for it, decides to take his medicine, as Wendy would want him to do.

Tinker Bell shrieks a warning, but Peter doesn't believe that Hook has poisoned the medicine, and he raises the cup to his lips to drink. Tinker Bell at once flies between him and the poison, drinks it all herself, and, to Peter's amazement, falls down almost immediately. Peter is saved, he now understands, but Tinker Bell is dying. It's at this point that Tink whispers she thinks she could get well if children believed in fairies, and Peter calls upon all children, including your own child, to clap their hands so Tinker Bell will live.

WHEN your child claps here, she's saying yes to the entire magic kingdom of Neverland, not only the fantasy but its connection to reality as well. And in doing so, she's giving her permission for it to live and to go on living.

It has been made very clear to us that the problems Peter must face—the kidnapping, the poisoning—developed because he selfishly broke off his partnership with Wendy, rejecting her vision of adulthood and home. This is the result of never wanting to grow up.

But after Peter has determined to make himself safe by turning his back on everything except the here and now and to stay in Neverland, he finds that even *that* is suddenly in jeopardy. To save his world, Peter has to do what he refused to do before—make an imaginative connection with the outside world, with *us*.

And for this essential moment, your child takes Wendy's place and holds open the door between Neverland and our world, maintaining the bond between fantasy and reality. It's a crucial challenge, one worthy the ruler of a magic kingdom.

YOUR child saves Neverland spontaneously, without even thinking, clapping in instinctive response to Peter's request. Like every hero of the magic kingdom, your child doesn't need to puzzle over the right thing to do or ponder what's good or what's bad. A challenge no sooner appears than the child-hero has answered, and the victory is won.

Captain Hook, in contrast, has no good, reliable instincts. He is a villain consumed by elaborate plans and brooding thoughts of revenge, but when the moment of truth comes, he falters, undone by the spontaneous Peter Pan.

Hook has been waiting for his opportunity to destroy Peter ever since he lost his right arm in a fight with the boy. The hook that replaced it has given the captain what is now his favorite weapon, but Peter threw the arm itself to a crocodile, who so enjoyed the taste that he has been following the pirate ever since, hoping to eat the rest of him. So far, Hook has been able to elude that fate only because the animal also swallowed a clock, whose loud ticking warns all around of the crocodile's approach.

Hook and his pirate crew have already tried to kill Peter and the Lost Boys with a poisoned cake, left out prominently to tempt the children to gorge themselves. This plan might have worked, but Wendy has more than once prevented the boys from eating the cake, because, she firmly explains, it's so "rich and damp" and bad for the digestion.

To Hook's despair, while Peter and the boys have Wendy to guide them, they are safe from the pirates' schemes. Smee, Hook's lieutenant, suggests that if the pirates kidnap Wendy and make her *their* mother, then the coast will be clear to go after Peter. So when Wendy and the boys climb out of their underground home, they are taken by Hook's men—Wendy to be the mother of the pirates, the boys to turn pirate or else walk the plank.

Villain that he is, Hook himself poisons Peter's medicine, since the boy now has no mother to prevent it. With his enemy presumed dead, the Lost Boys taken prisoner, and Wendy under guard, Hook should be celebrating the hour of his greatest triumph back at the pirate ship, but instead we find him silent and morose, hating the company of his pirate crew, who obey him out of fear. The plan has gone precisely as it should, he has done everything right, but Hook feels all wrong—all alone—and can't enjoy his accomplishments as any true pirate would.

* * *

OF course, Neverland's pirates aren't "true" pirates in the strictest sense, but rather the creation of a child's imagination, just like the rest of the island. They are children's dreams come to life, and naturally they show the unmistakable marks of a child's experiences and interests. One of Hook's pirates was an usher in a boys' school, another bears the incongruously commonplace name "Alf Mason," while piratical enemies are called "Barbecue" or "the Seacook." And Smee, the pirate lieutenant, busily occupies himself with his sewing on a perfectly ordinary machine, since *someone,* it seems, must keep the pirates' clothes in good repair.

These pirates, we soon see, are very middle-class indeed. Like the bourgeois buccaneers of Gilbert and Sullivan's *The Pirates of Penzance,* who celebrate with sips of sherry rather than swigs of rum, and plot to marry rather than carry off General Stanley's daughters, the pirates of Neverland never stray too far from the orderly, basically good-natured, and well-adjusted consciousness that created them.

The only truly sinister one among them is Captain Hook himself, and even his dark character is cast in schoolboy terms. This pirate captain isn't so much a monster as a bully, not so much a demon as a snob. But Hook is every schoolchild's nemesis—that classmate or teacher who sneers and gloats and preys upon the weak. He is a villain who looms large in a child's world, and for that reason, his downfall is particularly satisfying.

Of course, it's Peter Pan who beats Hook in a swordfight and sends him overboard to the waiting crocodile, but in a sense it's Hook who defeats himself from the beginning. In his hour of triumph, when Wendy and the boys are prisoners on board the pirate ship, when Peter is presumed poisoned, Hook is sullen and cast down, because, despite his power over the children, power even of life and death, he doesn't have the power to evoke their love, and, as he bitterly laments, "That's where the canker gnaws."

Here is where your child witnesses the real defeat of Captain Hook. Convinced of his superiority by virtue of his social prestige—Hook went to high-toned Eton, we discover—he is nevertheless tortured by self-doubt. It is the secret fear of every bully who builds himself up by belittling others, and here, in Neverland, your child sees it dramatically, hilariously revealed. The swaggering captain, who boasts of his piratical conquests and rules his ship with his deadly hook, moans and glowers because—of all things—he goes unloved, and worse, he's beginning to suspect that he deserves it.

HOOK is in this miserable frame of mind when the boys are brought before him on deck. He announces his intention to allow two of them to join the pirate crew, while the others will be forced to walk the plank. Who's it to be? Hook demands to know. Who will be a pirate, and who will die?

But instead of trembling with fear, the boys seem rather diffident in their reply, telling the Captain that they'll have to think about it because there are important aspects to consider. Would they be allowed to choose their own nicknames, for instance? Then, they ask one another, would their mothers approve? And what about their good standing as British subjects?

Infuriated by their chatter, Hook seizes the opportunity to say something villainous. With macabre enjoyment he hisses, "You would have to swear 'Down with the King!' " But his melodramatic pose is immediately deflated when the boys, in moral indignation at Hook's pronouncement, cry out to the frustrated captain, "Rule Britannia!"

Determined, at the very least, to be able to intimidate the young girl, Hook has Wendy brought up on deck and, sneering, unfolds to her his dastardly plan to do away with all the boys. But Wendy doesn't gratify him, and her coolness unnerves Hook even further, especially when he realizes she is staring with disdain at a spot on his shirt.

Already outdone in the matter of calm courage by the boys and Wendy, Hook's downfall is at hand. Suddenly he hears a ticking alongside the ship—surely his enemy, the crocodile—and in a panic begs the crew to hide him. The boys peer over the side, thinking to watch the crocodile climb aboard, and then realize it's actually Peter making the ticking sound, coming to their rescue. A wonderful trick, they conclude.

But, significantly, Peter didn't mean for it to happen as it did. While making his way through the forest, he'd ticked like the crocodile in order to pass by the watchful wild animals undetected. He'd intended then to climb aboard the pirate ship silently, and had in fact thought he'd done so, before he was struck by the pirates' amazement and the boys' admiration. By accident, he hadn't stopped ticking after all, but his carelessness turns out to have the same effect as ingenuity, and in the end he makes his way safely aboard to carry out the rescue.

IT is just this quality in Peter that drives Hook mad, and finally, in the duel the two fight aboard ship, it is what causes the pirate to go down to defeat. Hook plots meticulously, but Peter follows his instincts, and even his mistakes turn to his advantage. Hook leaves nothing to chance, but Peter relies on his luck, and it never fails him. So, when they face each other at last, all of the pirate's studied techniques are no match for Peter's spirit, because Hook can never hope to learn by rote what Peter knows by heart.

Before destroying Hook, Peter remakes the broken bond between himself and Wendy in a way that is characteristically both playful and imaginative. Without being seen by the pirates, Peter takes Wendy's place by the mast, concealed by her cloak. When Hook turns to order that the girl be cast overboard, Peter suddenly throws back the cloak, revealing himself and raising his sword against the pirate captain.

It's a wonderfully dramatic moment, of course, one your child will love re-creating in play. Here Peter and Wendy—

fantasy and reality—are one, and, as one, face Hook for the last time, sending him overboard to the crocodile, and to his doom. And in this victory over the very unhappy Hook, your own child realizes "the very pinnacle of good form."

"Good form" is Hook's phrase, schoolboy slang for that certain indefinable quality Peter possesses, a unique combination of courage, common sense, and unconscious grace. It's this same "good form" that Wendy and the boys show when Hook tries to frighten them, and, in fact, it's the same gratifying quality that most accurately defines all the heroes and heroines of the magic kingdom.

And let's not forget who single-handedly saves Neverland when its fairy light seems almost ready to go out entirely. Your child shares this royal attribute with all the rulers of the magic kingdom, and triumphs through imagination whenever they win the day.

THE bond forged in Neverland between fantasy and reality has triumphed over evil, and now it makes possible the return to London. The pirate ship, with the Lost Boys as crew and Peter as captain, sails on the wind through the night, away from Neverland and back to the Darlings' nursery window, which is open, just as Wendy has always promised it would be.

At the last moment, though, that open window hits a sore spot with Peter, and he and Tinker Bell fly ahead to try to bar the window so Wendy will have to fly back to Neverland. But the sight of Mrs. Darling inside, tears in her eyes, waiting hopefully for the return of her children, weakens Peter's resolve, and he allows the window to remain as it is, open and inviting.

When Wendy and her brothers are happily reunited with their parents, who blissfully agree to adopt all the Lost Boys, Peter is the only one on the outside, looking in at them through the window. He is barred from the group by his own refusal to accept change—to grow up.

* * *

IT is now that your child begins to realize that Wendy is going to have the best of both worlds in a way that Peter never will. Because Wendy is going to grow up, here in London, and will keep the child in her alive forever through the bond created in Neverland, she will experience joys that Peter, who won't grow up, will never know.

By accepting change, Wendy does grow up to be a happy young woman. She and the boys forget how to fly, but that magic is replaced by another, equally powerful magic, when time itself starts to fly. Wendy has a daughter, Jane, and tells her the story of Peter Pan and the adventures she had in Neverland long ago. And as if the tale itself were a conjuring, Peter Pan suddenly appears at the nursery window and Jane leaves with him for Neverland, just as Wendy once did.

So the crown of the magic kingdom is passed down from mother to daughter. Jane, we know, will rule over Neverland as queen-mother, then return to the world of London and grow up. And like her mother, she will retain that spark of childhood imagination, and will pass the magic on to a child of her own, just as you present your own child with the same royal legacy when you read with her the books you loved as a child—those stories of the magic kingdom that helped you to grow up while remaining in spirit, and in all the best ways, a child.

THE magic kingdom opens its door to a child and offers a crown, the prize to be won through courage, intelligence, and sympathy. After the victory, the child must leave the magic kingdom, but the success gained there is a promise of success in life, where the strengths and virtues of the growing child-hero will also be acknowledged and rewarded.

Sometimes the magic kingdom bestows a gift, a power—like flying—that lasts while the child stays within the landscape of imagination. Upon the return to ordinary life, the magic gift disappears, but it is replaced by something of greater value that will endure through life and never be taken away. Just as the crown of the magic kingdom is the symbol of a triumph that looks forward to the triumph of growing up, the magic gift is the promise of a true gift, one that is real and lasting.

In *Mary Poppins,* Jane and Michael fly to the ceiling and laugh with Uncle Albert, overcome with delight at the wonderful, uproarious time they're having. At the end of the afternoon, at Mary Poppins's command, the flying tea party ends, and the children's feet are back on solid ground. On the bus home, Jane and Michael begin to wonder if they really did fly, because Mary Poppins, as is her habit, refuses to discuss their magical adventures afterward, even to confirm that they have indeed happened. The flying is over, but two painfully shy children have started to enjoy meeting people, and they can feel happy and at ease in the company of others. Their feet are on the ground, but their spirits remain high and ebullient, an afternoon's flying turned into soaring confidence for a lifetime.

After they leave Neverland, Wendy, her brothers, and the Lost Boys forget how to fly, but they all grow up to be happy adults. And Wendy's favorite fantasy in Neverland—being a mother with a child to tell stories to—comes true in London. In return for ending her own flying adventure and coming home to grow up, Wendy is able to pass it on to her daughter, so that in a sense, Neverland never really ends for her.

A flight of imagination is a liberating experience. A child is suddenly free, able to move effortlessly and independently anywhere she wants. She is able to see much more, too, from above. Just as Christopher Robin, from his privileged perspective in the branches of a tree, watches Pooh and Piglet and sees that they're actually tracking themselves, a child who looks over the world while flying understands connections and meanings that are impossible to see on the ground. It is only from above that the real shape of the world can be seen.

* * *

FOR your child, some of the earliest visions of the shape of the world and of life itself come from the books you share together. Like the pirate ship that flies the children home in *Peter Pan,* these books will take your child on flights of imagination through fantasy into reality.

One of my favorite books as a child was *The Ship That Flew,* by Hilda Lewis. In this story of flying through space and time, the four Grant children discover a magic ship that comes to them under strange circumstances, almost as if it had searched them out. The ship starts out small, no bigger than a toy, but the children soon discover that it can grow large enough to hold all of them, and that it can take them by air anywhere they want to go. All they have to do is choose a place, and they can be there.

In this flying ship, the whole world becomes a magic kingdom for the children, the landscape of imagination laid out below them like a huge map, with adventure and challenge everywhere. In the ship, they can travel to other countries, learning geography by watching the world itself pass below them and learning firsthand the languages and customs of the places they visit. In fact, flying in this book seems very much like reading itself, an enactment of cultural literacy in its truest and most imaginative sense.

IT is the eldest child, Peter, who finds the wooden Viking ship in an old curiosity shop in an English seaside town, on a street he doesn't remember seeing before. Although he's almost sure he can't afford such a beautiful ship, he feels he must have it. Peter asks the old shopkeeper the price of the toy ship, and is told that its cost is "all the money you have in the world—and a bit over." The boy empties his pocket of all the money he has, including his bus fare home and the change he owes his father, and carries the ship away, hardly believing it is really his.

On the walk home, Peter tries a shortcut across the ocean

sands and suddenly finds that the tide is rushing in, threatening to drown him. Terrified, he wishes aloud that he were home, and immediately the toy ship begins to expand, growing large enough for him to get inside. He stands at the prow, while the ship rises in the air, flying swiftly above the sea and the cliffs to land gently outside his house.

Peter has always believed that magic existed, and wished that someday it would happen to him. Now it seems his wish has come true. But suddenly, after showing the ship's magic to his younger brother and sisters, Peter is struck with a terrible thought. What if the ship came to him by mistake, the strange old man in the shop selling it without really knowing what it was? Worried, the children return to town in the flying ship and search the streets for the shop, but they can't find it. Then they decide the ship must have been meant to be found by Peter—that it somehow *found him*—and so they will use the magic as they choose, secretly.

IN their flying ship, the children find that they can travel to other countries, and even, they discover, to other times. The customs and the language of each time and place they visit come to them magically when they touch the golden boar's head, so that their flying voyages teach them what we now call cultural literacy.

Sometimes the ship itself seems to be guiding them to certain times and places, as if it were their destiny. While the children are exploring the tombs of Egypt, for example, an archaeologist points out to them a curious message on a temple column, something about King Amenemhat I being saved by four gods in a flying ship.

Responding to the challenge, the four children travel to ancient Egypt, where a young prince, Usertsen, asks them for help in foiling a treacherous plot against his father, the king. The children use their flying ship to take the prince to warn his father of the trap laid for him, transport the king's troops to a decisive battle, and then return their royal friend safely to the palace. Before they part, the prince promises to honor their valor with a special inscription on a temple column—the message in hieroglyphics shown to them by the archaeologist.

The children learn history by literally becoming part of it. In fact, after journeying back and forth in time, meeting both famous and unknown people from every era, and actually witnessing events like the signing of Magna Carta and traveling with Chaucer on the pilgrimage to Canterbury, the children find that "the story of their country became a living, glowing world to them"—a magic kingdom, not only for the Grant children but for your child as well, where personal experience and imagination combine to make possible growth and understanding.

THE flying ship is indeed the children's key to the magic kingdom. Knowledge of the past, your child sees, brings a special meaning to the present, and sometimes reveals surprising power and beauty where we don't expect it.

On one of their early journeys, to Asgard, the realm of the Norse gods, the children learn of the ship's mystic origins and encounter its previous owner, mighty Frey, who, in a fury, demands it back. Peter refuses, but Odin, father of the gods, strikes a bargain to which everyone agrees. When the children grow tired of the magic ship, they will return it, and in exchange Odin will grant each child a wish.

By the end of five years, after many adventures, the children begin to outgrow the flying ship and doubt its magic. Although they remember their experiences—the panoply of history spread before them like a map—they can't remember if it all actually happened, or if their adventures were simply stories that Peter told them.

Peter knows the inevitable has happened. He commands the ship for the last time, telling it to take him back to the shop where he first saw it. There, Peter hands the ship back to the old man who sold it to him, recognizing him now as

Odin himself, and the god congratulates him on his good use of the ship and its magic.

Odin's promise to grant the children's wishes is faithfully kept, as such promises always are in the magic kingdom. When the ship's magic passes out of the children's lives, another kind of magic quietly replaces it. The brothers and sisters grow up and find their life's work in writing, archaeology, teaching, and medicine. And the happiness and success they enjoy in their professional work is Odin's gift, the magical legacy of their journeys in the ship that flew.

IN their flying ship, the Grant children travel the world and discover the importance of history, geography, archaeology, literature, art, and science. Their adventure is learning, and their learning is always an adventure, both wonderful and practical.

Because the flying ship frees the children to think with as much delight as they play, their childhood imagination lives on in their adulthood. Their play as children naturally evolves into their adult work, giving a unity to their lives that really does seem as magical as a gift from a god.

In reading the stories of the magic kingdom with your own child, you're giving him a gift that will help him to grow and face all the challenges of life. It's a magic that makes learning the secret languages of history and literature, the arts and sciences, an adventure—a flight of imagination over an ever wider and more fascinating world.

CHAPTER SIX

New Worlds Ahead

You read to your child from the time she's a baby to show her the magic that lives in a book. You hold her on your lap and open up a world before her, with beautiful landscapes to explore and exciting adventures to experience. The time you spend reading together seems happy enough to be an end in itself, but the fact is that enjoying books on a parent's lap teaches a child lessons in reading that can't be found anywhere else. True literacy—real fluency in reading—doesn't come from flash cards, but from love and imagination.

The first time I saw Franny reading a book on her own, one she had chosen herself, I must confess I was a little nostalgic, as well as proud. Certainly I'd hoped for this moment—imagined it, relished the thought of it—just as I'd once longed for the day she would speak her first words, or take her first steps. All the reading we had enjoyed together had been in preparation for this, her first solo flight of imagination. I was delighted that her skill was strong enough to see her through pages and pages, both easy and difficult passages, all by herself.

From now on, I told myself, Franny could decide to read a book whenever she wanted without any help. I had given her a magical gift, and now she had, in turn, marked a great accomplishment, the result of time, love, and shared wonder. I wouldn't wish it otherwise for worlds, but still, I was a little sad because, as I saw it, a part of her childhood—a part I had enjoyed more than I knew—had come to an end.

Of course, I soon came to realize that reading to my child wasn't a thing of the past at all. When Franny wasn't busy with her own reading, we still found time to read together those books just beyond the range of her fluency. And I enjoyed it just as much, but differently. Instead of a student, I now had a partner, who, at times, would take a turn reading to *me*.

On her own, Franny soon made her way through many of

the books I'd loved as a child. Some of them we had explored together years before, and some were entirely new to her. Of the books we'd read together first, she told me that the characters, the plots, even certain descriptions seemed familiar, but different somehow, now that she was reading on her own. When she thought of the Alice story she'd heard read by me and the Alice story she was now reading, the two blended in her mind, and seemed, she told me, suddenly to come alive for her.

I had been with Franny the first time through Wonderland and the Looking-Glass World, but she discovered her way to Narnia all on her own, without my help at all. One day I found her with *The Lion, the Witch and the Wardrobe,* the book opened nearly at the middle. And Franny herself was deeply engaged in what she was reading, off in another world—one I remembered well from my own childhood. It had been years since I'd been there, but, as you know, once a queen in Narnia, always a queen in Narnia.

All the books of the magic kingdom show your child ingenious ways to pass from one world to another, whether through a wardrobe or a mirror, out the nursery window, or down a rabbit-hole. Their purpose is to help her make that equally challenging passage through time, from childhood through adolescence and then on to adulthood. Don't be afraid, these stories say, just be yourself. And when you look around, you'll find magic.

TIME and growth move your child always forward, toward life in the grown-up world. However wonderful and exciting any stage of childhood is, it can never be repeated. No one can go back, but the incentive to go forward is strengthened by the realization that even more wonderful and adventurous times lie ahead.

In one of the later adventures in Narnia, Lucy finds a magic book full of spells and surprises. Turning the large, colorful pages, she wonders at the extraordinary powers it promises a reader—the ability to find buried treasure, to know if someone is lying, to hear what is said about you when you're not there. The more she reads, the more exciting the spells and beautiful the pictures.

Then Lucy turns to a page that begins a spell "for the refreshment of the spirit," but as she reads, she discovers it's not so much a spell as a story. In fact, it's the most wonderful story she's ever read. She reads on, page after page, in utter fascination, and realizes with a start that she can't remember what she's been reading. When she tries to return to the beginning of the story, she finds that the pages of the magic book can't be turned back, only forward.

Lucy's magic story is a bit like childhood itself, so fun and exciting as we live it that we sometimes forget to notice its larger patterns. Still, when memory fails, the heart remembers in its own way. And years later, whenever Lucy calls a story "good," she means that it reminds her of the story in the magic book she once read, but now can't quite remember.

Early in childhood, the stories of the magic kingdom help your child to put aside the toys and rituals of the nursery to make way for the challenges of friendship, school, and independence. Later on, as your child begins to feel the awakenings of adolescence and that irresistible impetus to move forward in life, out into the larger world, the magic kingdom offers a vision of what lies ahead. As he reads, your child can imagine himself grown-up already, an adult acting responsibly, even heroically, in a world as large as life.

THE fully realized "secondary world" of fantasy, as J. R. R. Tolkien has called it, includes a detailed cosmology, an imaginative anthropology, and even an alternate history. In such magic kingdoms as Narnia and Middle-earth, your child witnesses history unfold, civilizations rise and fall, wars fought and averted, and, in light of these fictional worlds, begins to think about the ways the real world works, and what part she might play in it as an adult.

The creators of Middle-earth and Narnia, Tolkien and C. S. Lewis, were close friends and colleagues, and, like Lewis Carroll, dreamed their worlds into being while teaching at Oxford, that cradle of magic kingdoms. With their separate series, *The Lord of the Rings* and *The Chronicles of Narnia,* Tolkien and Lewis create stories that intrigue adults as well as children, while at the same time opening up exciting new possibilities for all fantasy by presenting traditional mythic characters and themes with a contemporary sensibility. Elves, fauns, and dragons become novel and interesting once more, even modern, in their way.

In bringing to life again the creatures and quests of folktales and sagas, stories from the earliest forms of fiction, Tolkien and Lewis together affirm that the imagination of childhood does not fade in adolescence. Just as myths from the childhood of the world can be remade to express ideas in modern times, the awe and wonder we feel as children, in hearing or reading fantasy, can—and should be—rekindled to light the path to adulthood.

IT's no surprise that for Tolkien, who was a scholar specializing in Anglo-Saxon, the most fascinating task in creating a "secondary world" was the invention of its languages. As *The Lord of the Rings* unfolds, we are offered phrases, brief conversations, and even poetry in the different languages of elves, dwarves, and orcs, and Tolkien's philological creativity has such integrity that we can tell each language from the others in a matter of words.

Along with his word-craft, Tolkien possesses the gift for evoking an entire world through the description of a riverbank or a path through a grassy meadow—imaginary landscapes most often pastoral but with a palpable immediacy to them—and the source of his strength lies in childhood memory. At three, when Tolkien arrived in England with his parents from South Africa, where he was born in 1892, he saw for the first time the English countryside—green and hilly—and this impression, he later explained, stayed with him all his life. And it is from that childhood memory that he formed the landscape of Middle-earth.

In the beginning, Tolkien told his stories of Middle-earth to his young children as he thought of them, and later, when he began to write them down as *The Lord of the Rings,* he read the manuscript-in-progress to a small circle of fellow writers in Oxford who met weekly. "The Inklings," as they called themselves, delighted in food, drink, and the well-filled pipe, and they enjoyed the "hobbit-books" so much that Tolkien dedicated *The Fellowship of the Ring* to the group, adding that their enthusiasm for the tale made him wonder if they were in fact descended from the hobbits themselves.

THE Inkling who most admired Tolkien's "hobbit-books" was C. S. Lewis, a professor of Renaissance literature as well as a popular writer and speaker on Christianity. Possibly in emulation of Tolkien, Lewis wrote his own multivolume tale of another world, *The Chronicles of Narnia.* Like Middle-earth, Narnia is a place populated by mythic creatures—dragons, dwarves, fauns—but it is different because it is a world created to be visited by children from our world, and the adventures of the children who travel there can be read, on one level, as an allegory of Christian mysteries.

The allegorical dimension of Narnia, with the lion Aslan as a Christ figure, was an important part of the fiction for Lewis, but if it had been the story's only meaning, *The Chronicles of Narnia* would never have achieved its great popularity. As it is, the values of Narnia, like those of Middle-earth, are universally acknowledged. Courage, truthfulness, love—the same virtues that appear in all the stories of the magic kingdom—are expressed through the child-heroes in Narnia, and the power of Aslan, though a theologian might define it as "grace," can also be called "imagination."

* * *

IN Narnia and Middle-earth, your child discovers a fully realized world, a magic kingdom that offers the landscape of
childhood imagination as well as the pathway to adulthood.
Tolkien creates Middle-earth out of vivid landscapes and languages, as well as a history that fills several appendices, and
the sheer volume of words—about a half a million in all—
gives us a palpable sense of an entire world. Lewis, on the
other hand, prefers to round out Narnia by a narrative sleight
of hand—the fortuitous detail that suddenly brings the whole
picture into three dimensions.

At the end of *The Magician's Nephew,* the sixth book in the
series, Lewis gives us a revealing glimpse into the origins of
his magic kingdom. The boy Digory leaves the newly created Narnia, your child learns, with the apple of youth that
will cure his dying mother, and after she eats it, the boy
buries the core in the backyard. From this seed, a tree
grows—a Narnian tree, stately and beautiful, though not as
powerful as the one growing in Narnia itself.

Its fruit won't restore life, but Digory firmly believes that
it does possess some magical qualities, so when a strong wind
knocks it down many years later, he doesn't burn its wood.
Instead, he has it carefully cut and made into a wardrobe.
And years after that, Digory—now the Professor—hosts the
four children who go exploring through his house, and it is
when they find this wardrobe that their adventures in Narnia
begin.

IT is through this very wardrobe that the children, and your
own child, find their original passageway to Narnia. The first
one through this door is Lucy, the youngest and most intu-
itive of the four, and what she discovers is a path of sensuous
surprise.

Alone in the spare room, she impulsively tries the wardrobe door just to see if it will open, and when she sees a row
of long fur coats hanging up, she steps inside—again impulsively—to feel the fur against her skin. Although it's very

dark, it's wonderful to pass between these smooth, soft coats that hang inside, first one row and then another.

Surrounded by quiet darkness and fur on all sides, Lucy steps carefully forward through the rows of coats, her hands in front of her, but she doesn't find the back of the wardrobe as she expects. Instead, just as she wonders how large and deep the wardrobe really is, she hears a crunching under her feet. Her first thoughts are of mothballs—she saw some roll out as she opened the wardrobe door—but when she reaches down to touch the floor, she finds it's covered with something cold. The fur around her face is now prickly, like the branches of trees, and suddenly she sees not the back of the wardrobe, or another row of coats, but a light, far off ahead of her.

Aware now of something falling all around her, soft and cold, Lucy realizes to her utter astonishment that she is no longer in the wardrobe, but in a wood at night during a snowfall. She recognizes the light ahead as quite an ordinary lamppost, but the figure approaching her, arms full of packages, isn't ordinary at all. It's a faun, and upon seeing Lucy he drops his packages, startled almost beyond speech at the sight of a "Daughter of Eve," an actual human child.

IN the true tradition of the magic kingdom, Lucy has followed her instincts and, like Alice, her curiosity has suddenly and magically unlocked another world. And once she's on her way, Lucy explores everything around her, learning through her senses just as children love to do.

The first bewildering truth that comes her way in the wardrobe is the Narnian paradox that the inside is actually bigger than the outside. Small as the wardrobe seems before Lucy steps in, it opens up magically to contain a lamppost, a wood, a faun, an entire world. And like your child's imagination, it grows and expands through learning and experience.

Lucy is a child who can imagine, and for this Narnia offers itself to her, awaiting the delight of her recognition. The first creature she sees, the faun who is nearly overcome by her importance, honors her with a festive tea. The evil White Witch has commanded all in Narnia to bring any human child to her at once, but Mr. Tumnus, his faun's heart touched by Lucy's kind nature and her interest in his world, decides to risk his life to keep her safe. Simply by being herself, Lucy has found the way not only to Narnia, but to Narnia's heart as well.

FROM the beginning, Narnia reveals itself to the child who is willing to see it, like Van Allsburg's sleigh bell that rings for those who believe. The power to enter this world through imagination—to create, in a sense, the magic kingdom of Narnia—belongs to all children. Lucy finds the way by opening a wardrobe door, your own child by opening the pages of a book.

Although Lewis was writing during the 1950s, he set *The Magician's Nephew*, the story of Aslan's creation of Narnia, back in the time "when your grandfather was a child"—the late Victorian era of Sherlock Holmes, gaslight, and horse-drawn cabs. Narnia, of course, has its own time, but Lewis dates it by our reckoning in the golden age of the magic kingdom tradition, when the *Alice* books were still current as well as popular, *The Wind in the Willows* the new classic, and *Peter Pan* a tremendous theatrical success.

It was a golden age for Lewis as well, the time of his own boyhood, and he describes the food, the clothes, the furnishings with the directness of a child speaking to other children. Even the play of Digory and Polly in the upper reaches of the row houses at the beginning of *The Magician's Nephew* re-creates the play that Lewis himself had enjoyed with his brother as a boy.

For his own manipulative purposes, Digory's Uncle Andrew, a magician of sorts, has been experimenting with some rings he believes may take the wearer into another world and then return him to ours again. The idea itself—being transported by magic—is wonderful, but because Uncle Andrew's motives and methods are evil, evil comes of his magic.

To prove his theory, Uncle Andrew sends Digory's friend Polly into another world without asking her or providing her with the ring to return, assuming that Digory will follow in order to rescue her. After some traveling back and forth between strange worlds, Digory and Polly return to the magician's study, inadvertently bringing with them Jadis, a witch who has destroyed her own world and seeks another one to rule. Digory and Polly use the rings to take the witch out of our world, and this time they are accompanied by Uncle Andrew and a London cabman as well.

The group finds itself in a silent, dark, and desolate world without life. The cabman, a friendly young fellow from the country, says out loud what the rest are thinking—perhaps they're dead. In that case, he proposes gamely, let's sing a hymn. He cheerily begins a harvest song of thanksgiving, and the children join in, while Uncle Andrew and the witch remain silent and sullen.

When they stop singing, they hear a great, beautiful voice singing as if in response to their hymn. The music goes on and on in the darkness, the voice swelling and growing as all of them, except Uncle Andrew and Jadis the witch, listen in delight. Then the one voice becomes many voices, and the stars, "a thousand, thousand points of light," suddenly appear in the sky all at once. They see hills on the horizon, and the one great voice swells triumphantly as a sun rises. Its first light reveals the First Voice, by far the most fascinating sight yet.

It is a Lion, and he paces majestically as he sings. His song, gentle and low now, fills the air, while around him grass appears, trees and flowers shoot up. Polly realizes that it is the Lion who is making all this happen, and that the world growing all around them is being created through his music.

Jadis, made furious by the Lion's music and his creation, hurls an iron bar she has wrenched from a London lamppost. The bar strikes the Lion in the face, but bounces off harmlessly. She runs away screaming, and the iron bar, which has landed in the grass, grows like a tree into a lamp-post, and will become one of the most important Narnian landmarks. And even Jadis herself is fated to play a part in Narnia's history, as the evil tyrant known to her subjects as the White Witch.

Now the Lion's song brings forth animals, churning out of the earth like bubbles in a boiling pot. The Lion walks among the animals, choosing two from each kind, and breathes on them. Those not chosen wander away, but the others start to grow and change—a sort of magical, high-speed evolution—and begin to look as if they want to understand what's happening. The Lion calls to the animals and to all his creation, "Narnia, Narnia, Narnia, awake." The children feel the power of the Lion's voice in their blood, and all around them Narnia comes to life.

The story of the creation of the world through music has biblical roots, and clearly Lewis means for us to see a connection. But Narnia isn't the world created in Genesis. Narnia is a magic kingdom, a realm of imagination where a child-hero can be challenged to grow and to rule. And so the song of creation doesn't begin with the Lion's song, but with the song of the children and their friend. It is in response to their spontaneous hymn that the great voice starts to sing.

Narnia exists because children imagine it. And in return for their belief, Narnia offers the crown of the magic kingdom, first to the cabman and his wife, who will be Narnia's Adam and Eve, and then to Peter, Susan, Edmund, and Lucy. Even if a child has brought trouble along, as Digory has, Narnia responds with a challenge, a great task to dispel the evil and to gain a hero's acclaim.

A child's imagination gives Narnia life, and Narnia, in kind, makes possible a life of imagination. Come and rule, Narnia calls to your child. Be among us and grow strong and wise. Live by the words Aslan spoke at this magic kingdom's birth: "Love. Think. Speak."

* * *

IN *The Last Battle,* the book that concludes *The Chronicles of Narnia,* Lewis brings his story to a close, but Narnia itself doesn't really end, because it will always live on in the imagination of children. In this last story, Lewis makes clear that Narnia depends on children for magic and power, just as Neverland—and, really, all the magic kingdoms—look to children to give them life.

Tirian, last of the Narnian kings, is captured by the enemy and bound to a tree. Alone in the cold and dark, with no chance of rescue or escape, he reflects on his country's long history and its present crisis. Narnia has passed through many dangerous times, but always, when hope seemed gone, the country had been saved by children who came from another world. Now, in the hour of greatest need, King Tirian calls out to the children who are friends of Narnia, and begs them to come to its rescue.

Suddenly, Tirian finds himself in a room where all those who have been kings, queens, and heroes of Narnia are sitting together at dinner. He sees Digory and Polly, now grown to be very old, who were present at Narnia's birth, and who traveled far to a garden for the seed of a tree to protect the land from evil. He sees the children who said they had come to Narnia through a wardrobe, and who joined Aslan in defeating the White Witch. And here also are the youngest two, Eustace and Jill, who saved Prince Rilian from evil enchantment.

All the child-heroes are gathered here together, and gaze at him, amazed, but when Tirian tries to speak, he discovers he can't. He awakens to find morning has come, and despairs that he has failed to summon the children. But then before him appear Jill and Eustace, the youngest friends of Narnia, who have come from their world by the power of Aslan.

The battle Jill and Eustace fight is Narnia's final struggle, the culmination of its history. But the end of Narnia is just the beginning of the New Narnia, on the other side of Aslan's door. All the children and their friends gather in a walled garden, marveling that the small space can hold so many. Then Lucy realizes that this secret garden manifests the same magic as the wardrobe she stepped into long ago—paradoxically, the inside is bigger than the outside. To enter it is to encounter nothing less than an entire world, as big as a child's imagination.

A secret garden can hold a world. A child—your own child—is a hero, ruler of the magic kingdom. Through all of the children's adventures in Narnia, Aslan's love and encouragement takes the form of a challenge. Before a quest or a battle, the Lion gently reminds his young friends that they aren't too little or too helpless to perform heroic deeds. In love and honor, Aslan calls the children who are friends of Narnia to be kings and queens—brave, generous, noble. The children answer the challenge, accomplish great deeds in Narnia, and return to our world confident, unafraid, grown-up.

IN Tolkien's Middle-earth, your child finds the same heroic story as in Narnia, but here it is a whole culture of people who are called upon to grow by facing the challenges of the magic kingdom. *The Hobbit* and *The Lord of the Rings* recount the mighty deeds of unlikely heroes, characters who reveal surprising inner strength and courage.

On the surface shy, small, and unassuming, Tolkien's heroes, as Lucy would say, are bigger on the inside. Like all the children of the magic kingdom, they surprise us—and themselves—with the bravery, nobility, and wisdom they possess. And they use these extraordinary powers to accomplish the greatest task, the greatest adventure life can offer. They grow up.

The story of *The Lord of the Rings* begins with *The Hobbit*, the tale of Bilbo Baggins's unexpected adventures among dwarves and dragons. Like Mole in *The Wind in the Willows*, Bilbo scurries up and out of his hole and runs toward the wider world without really knowing why. Bilbo journeys to

Rivendell, just as Mole makes his way to the River Bank, and finds the world more beautiful and exciting than he ever could have imagined back in his comfortable, narrow, little underground home. Without realizing it, Bilbo discovers a magic kingdom, where he meets challenges he once thought impossible, and he returns to his home a hero, confident, strong, and actually bigger and taller than before.

Tolkien's story grows directly out of the magic kingdom tradition, as well as the rich history of fantasy and folklore. Tolkien's unique contribution to the tradition is the creation of the hobbit race itself, which he places alongside the elves and the dwarves as another kind of imaginary creature, similar to humans in intelligence, emotions, and behavior.

In *The Lord of the Rings,* the elves are known for their genius for creating art and poetry, and the dwarves for their strength and fortitude in mining gold. The hobbits are fine storytellers and craftsmen, as the elves are, but hobbit art most often takes the form of carefully and simply prepared meals, and their poetry runs to songs about food and drink rather than love and war. Like the dwarves, whom they resemble, they live underground, but their chief concerns are comfort and security, not precious metal.

The hobbits are best known only for being homey. A hobbit-hole, like Bilbo's Bag End, is easily envisioned by a child who has been inside Mrs. Tittlemouse's tidy residence. Its domestic comforts as well as its name recall Mole End, another tranquil home left suddenly and unaccountably vacant.

In both *The Hobbit* and *The Fellowship of the Ring,* which is the first volume of the trilogy recounting the Ring Wars, Tolkien sketches out a physical description of his creatures that reveals much about the hobbits' character and their place in the world of Middle-earth. Hobbits are generally two to four feet tall, Tolkien tells us, slimmer and smaller than dwarves, but beardless. They love brightly colored clothing, go without shoes, and are skillful in keeping out of the sight of "the Big Folk." Their greatest enjoyments are eating, drinking, laughing, parties, and presents.

The other folk of Middle-earth refer to the hobbits as "halflings" or the "half-grown," and hobbit ways seem always to be a mystery to them. But the hobbits' appearance, their likes and dislikes, their values all make sense to us, and have an endearing, familiar quality. We recognize them as children, and we see that they give the unmistakable signs of growing up. The hobbits and their child-culture are about to come of age as a people in a world of ancient folkways.

THE story of *The Hobbit* is the adventure of someone who thought he would never have one, and was content that way. In a warm and playful tone that is especially delightful when read aloud, Tolkien presents Bilbo Baggins, a thoroughly ordinary, respectable hobbit, quite regular in his habits, whose life suddenly becomes complicated when a strange wizard named Gandalf knocks on his door and announces that he's looking for someone to go on an adventure. Bilbo makes polite excuses for declining, tries to get the wizard to leave, but finds instead that somehow he has invited Gandalf to tea the next day.

Bilbo remembers the invitation only when he hears a knock at the door at teatime, but it isn't Gandalf who has arrived. Instead, Bilbo finds dwarves filing in by twos and threes, and soon he's busy serving twelve guests when he had expected only one.

By the time Gandalf joins the group, teatime has become dinnertime, and Bilbo's company shows no sign of leaving. When, after their meal, the dwarves sing of their beloved gold, lost long ago to a dragon, Bilbo is strangely moved, and feels almost as if he would like to travel with the group and see the world outside the Shire.

Then Bilbo discovers that there is an agenda to this convocation. Suddenly, briskly, the dwarves turn to what they call "the business" of the evening, and begin to talk animatedly with Gandalf. As Bilbo listens, he realizes with a start that the dwarves are plotting to steal their gold back from the dragon, and that he, Bilbo, is expected to be the burglar.

Gandalf apparently sought the hobbit out and brought the dwarves to his house for that purpose.

There is more to Bilbo than even he knows, Gandalf announces to the dwarves and their astonished host. But when the hobbit wakes up the next morning, the strange talk of the night before seems very far away. The dwarves have left, and Bilbo's part in the adventure seems highly unlikely. Bilbo is quietly eating his breakfast when Gandalf arrives and shows him a note from his guests that Bilbo has overlooked. They are waiting at a nearby inn and expect Bilbo to join them by eleven at the latest. With ten minutes to make up his mind and to get to the meeting place, Bilbo is suddenly filled with energy. He runs out of his house, without his hat, money, or even a handkerchief, and arrives at the inn breathless at precisely eleven. Bilbo's "Tookish" side—the part he inherited from his mother's family, the adventurous Tooks—has come out in spite of his Baggins prudence.

Bilbo starts on this journey with some uncertainty, but gains resolve and strength along the way, finding within himself a surprising quantity of boldness, resourcefulness, sympathy, intelligence, and courage. Gandalf's judgment of him proves true after all. Bilbo slays the dragon and recovers the gold, and finds a magic ring that can make the wearer invisible. Especially pleased with this, his own lawful booty from the raid, Bilbo artfully tricks Gollum, the ring's owner, in order to keep it, and this, we'll later find, is the most significant event of the entire expedition.

A year later, Bilbo returns to his home rich, happy, and, most of all, grown. Going out into the wider world and taking on its dangers is a greater adventure than he ever realized. And in realizing the adventure, in rising to its challenges, Bilbo realizes himself.

WITH *The Fellowship of the Ring, The Two Towers,* and *The Return of the King,* Tolkien's story of Middle-earth takes on a quality different from the simple excitement and adventure of

The Hobbit. The tone of the narration in this trilogy does not recall a comfortable bedtime story, and the plot grows in complexity as it unfolds, but your child will recognize the same essential story of a child-hero who must face crucial challenges in order to keep hope alive in a magic kingdom.

Frodo, Bilbo's nephew, is the hero this time, and his adventure follows the same pattern as his uncle's—"there and back again"—but for much higher stakes than the recovery of stolen gold. Frodo, like Bilbo, is called unexpectedly to set out on a road he has never before traveled, but while Bilbo's summons is an invitation to explore the world, Frodo's is a command to save it.

When Bilbo, in a green old age, leaves the Shire to live quietly in Rivendell, Frodo, as his heir, receives Bag End, with its comfortable furnishings and, most important, the magic ring Bilbo stole from Gollum. This ring, Gandalf explains, is not the harmless trinket it seemed when Bilbo first put it on and found that it made him invisible. It is a ring of power—indeed, *the* Ring of Power—created by the Dark Lord Sauron as a means of controlling every creature in Middle-earth.

Although Bilbo wasn't aware of it, he was under the Ring's power all the time he had it—or, as Gandalf insists, for the time it had him. Bilbo had grown as a result of his adventure, but it is in the nature of the Ring of Power to arrest the growth of its wearer, while at the same time holding off death. To possess the Ring, therefore, is to stagnate, neither growing nor dying, but dwindling to a shade.

Moreover, the Ring turns its wearer to evil, and the more powerful the impulse to control it, the greater the evil. For this reason Gandalf, a powerful wizard, won't dare touch the Ring, for fear he would turn into another Dark Lord. But Bilbo, because of his humility and goodness, has escaped this fate, and has even managed with some difficulty to pass the Ring willingly on to someone else, something that has never happened before.

Now Frodo has the Ring and stands in peril of wasting

away or becoming evil. And the whole Shire, too, is in danger, because the Dark Lord has discovered where the Ring is, and he is determined to retrieve it. If the Ring returns to its evil creator, all of Middle-earth will be the slaves of Sauron, with no beauty, light, or freedom anywhere. To prevent this, Gandalf tells Frodo the Ring must be destroyed by the fire that made it, in the Cracks of Doom in Mordor, the realm of the Dark Lord himself.

How all this is to be accomplished even Gandalf himself cannot predict. What is clear is that for the safety of the Shire, the Ring must be taken far away, and for the safety of Middle-earth, it must somehow be destroyed. Because Frodo has the Ring, the responsibility for taking the first step must be his.

Although he wonders why he was chosen, Frodo never refuses his destiny. Clearly, he has been called on a quest into the larger world, outside the Shire, to face a challenge that has crucial consequences for all of Middle-earth and all of history. Frodo is called into a world in peril, to fight evil and stagnation, and to bring back hope. And the prize that awaits the hero of the adventure in this magic kingdom is growth, not just for himself, but for his people, and for his entire world.

WITH Frodo's quest, the tradition of the magic kingdom that you and your child have charted from the earliest books reaches a universal level. Now the imaginary land encompasses an entire world, and the challenge the child-hero must face is the rescue of civilization itself. Yet in spite of these enormous stakes, *The Lord of the Rings* presents virtually the same drama as the *Pooh* and *Alice* books, *The Secret Garden*, and *The Wind in the Willows*.

In all these stories, a child unexpectedly enters a new world, different and exciting, and through courage, intelligence, and natural nobility, faces its challenges and becomes its hero and ruler. Alice looking over the checkerboard landscape of the Looking-Glass World, Christopher Robin opening the green door to answer the needs of his Forest friends, Mary Lennox surveying her secret garden for the first time and deciding to take on the responsibility of bringing it back to life—each of these children, like Frodo, sees a world that calls for heroic action, and each answers that call spontaneously and freely.

Every child-hero of the magic kingdom, just like your own child, finds the inner strength to meet the challenges of a new world, and in imagination prepares for the adventure that awaits in reality—the adventure of growing up and entering the adult world.

This is now Frodo's destiny. Gandalf advises him to leave the Shire soon, with his servant Sam, and to make for Rivendell, where the ancient, wise elf Elrond may be able to counsel him further. When the hobbits arrive, including Merry and Pippin, Frodo's cousins, they find that many other travelers have gathered there—not only elves, but men, dwarves, and the wizard Gandalf, too. Elrond has called the representatives of the free peoples to council, to decide how they will face their common danger.

The Dark Lord's power is moving all through Middle-earth by means of his evil servants, the Black Riders, and they are searching for a mysterious ring. At the same time, war between Sauron's kingdom, Mordor, and Gondor, the kingdom of men, has begun. Boromir, son of the Steward of Gondor, tells of a strange dream commanding him to "seek for the Sword that was broken," warning of "Isildur's Bane," and concluding enigmatically that "the Halfling forth shall stand."

Boromir has come to Rivendell to hear Elrond's interpretation of the dream. But before Elrond can speak, the man Aragorn rises and solves the riddle. The sword that was broken is the symbol of the true king of Gondor—Aragorn shows it as proof of his kingship—and it shall be reforged for war, according to ancient prophecy, when Isildur's Bane is found.

And Isildur's Bane *has* been found. Gandalf instructs Frodo to show the council the Ring. With this, the conclusion of the prophetic dream is realized—the "Halfling," or hobbit, has come forward, and is recognized for the first time in the council of the mighty and the wise.

"THE Halfling forth shall stand"—the prophecy fulfilled at the Council of Elrond when Frodo reveals the Ring to the assembled free peoples—foretells an individual's initiation into power, but it also speaks of the emergence of all the hobbit-folk from their obscurity. Now the hobbits, represented by Frodo and Bilbo, are seated with the most powerful and ancient peoples of Middle-earth—elves, dwarves, and men—as equals, to discuss war and peace, good and evil. And the smallest, most childlike of the group has brought to the table a power that is unequaled—a Ring that may bring an end to history.

Frodo sits, quiet and a little self-conscious, as the leaders of Middle-earth discuss the Ring and possible strategies for defense against the forces of Mordor. With emotion, and barely checked by civility, they debate among themselves. What were once philosophical issues are now practical questions. Can a power made by evil do any good? Can an evil power like the Ring's be controlled without corruption? What sacrifices should be made for war? For peace?

At last, with difficulty, they decide that the war against Mordor, however perilous, must be fought without using the power of the Ring, and that the Ring must be destroyed in the fires of Mount Doom. Someone, then, must take the Ring to the Cracks of Doom, but the strongest and wisest would be most susceptible to the Ring's evil power. Gandalf tells the council that the once-great wizard, Saruman the White, has been corrupted by Sauron. Had Saruman been trusted with the Ring, all of Middle-earth would have been lost already. For the great leaders, the temptation to seize the Ring's power would be irresistible.

In the face of this dilemma, the wise Elrond muses that

small hands turn some wheels as ably as the hands of the mighty. The task, it seems, is destined to be undertaken by someone who would not be the obvious choice. A long silence follows at the table, and then Frodo is surprised to hear his own voice in response. "I will take the Ring," Frodo says, "though I do not know the way."

With this brief speech, Frodo takes upon himself the most perilous challenge of the magic kingdom, and it comes to him because, of all the company present, he is most like a child. Elrond accepts Frodo's offer gratefully, declaring that this crucial point in history, with the world poised on the brink of ruin or rebirth, is "the hour of the Shire-folk," the hobbits' chance to take their place beside men, elves, and dwarves, and, with the free peoples, to endure and to fight to save Middle-earth.

AT Rivendell, your child's imaginative identification with Frodo is rewarded with the approval of the Council of Elrond, the gathering of the most powerful individuals in Middle-earth. Frodo wins their admiration and respect simply by being himself, by responding spontaneously to an instinct even he can't fully understand.

In accepting the responsibility for taking the Ring to Mordor, Frodo suddenly speaks his heart. What's inside him—his truest self—is clearly expressed before he is even aware it's happening, and in a moment he finds himself in the center of action at a time of crisis. He has stood up before the world and announced that he's ready to take on a heroic challenge.

Now everyone is looking to Frodo to follow through, to be a hero. Frodo will bear the Ring, but Elrond decrees that the hobbit will not face the power of Mordor without companions. The burden will be taken up in fellowship, with representatives from all the free peoples of Middle-earth, since the peril is one that endangers them all.

The company is chosen both for strength and for distinction. So when Frodo the Ringbearer leaves Rivendell for

[173]

Mordor, he is accompanied by Gandalf the wizard; Boromir and Aragorn, both men; Gimli the dwarf; Legolas the elf; and three other hobbits—his servant, Sam, and his young cousins, Merry and Pippin. Sam, Merry, and Pippin have not so much might to offer, but Elrond concedes that their love for Frodo is itself a kind of power.

THE stories of the magic kingdom often involve a group of children, usually brothers and sisters, who travel on adventures together. The hobbit contingent, four of the nine members of the Fellowship of the Ring, works the same way. Each of them is important, although different, and all of them, from the oldest to the youngest, hold your child's attention and affection.

On the journey, each of the hobbits proves his own worth as well as the valor of his people. As Elrond declared in the council, this is the hour of the Shire-folk, and Sam, Merry, and Pippin, as well as Frodo, take part in defeating the powers of evil.

So, although Frodo is the central hero of this magic kingdom, there are three other characters whom your child can cheer on. Sam, Merry, and Pippin are the younger members of the hobbit group—little brothers, in a way—but they will prove their intelligence, courage, and nobility just the same as Frodo.

Not long after the company leaves Rivendell, Merry and Pippin get their opportunity to prove their mettle on this adventure. Separated from the rest of the group, they are suddenly attacked by the goblinlike Orcs, who are in the service of the evil wizard Saruman. They are roughly treated by the Orcs, kept alive only because Saruman believes they may be carrying the Ring.

Merry and Pippin keep their heads throughout their captivity, and when they hear that the Orcs are after the Ring, Pippin comes up with a plan to use their captors' greed to their advantage. Promising to hand over the Ring, they ask to be untied, and then make their escape in the confusion when the Orcs are suddenly attacked by the Riders of Rohan.

After their getaway, Merry and Pippin talk together lightly and casually, as if they hadn't been through anything more than an inconvenience. It is this calm attitude—Captain Hook would call it "good form without knowing it"—that brings them the good fortune to meet and impress a powerful ally for the free peoples of Middle-earth.

Merry and Pippin are walking through the wood, looking for the rest of their company, when they are found by Treebeard, the Ent, an ancient, mighty herder of trees. Although he distrusts most creatures, Treebeard is pleased by Merry's and Pippin's clear but gentle voices and by the courtesy they show him, and he offers them food and shelter.

The hobbits show their respect for Treebeard's Entish insistence on slow and careful speech and, according to their host's custom, they unfold the story of their travels, without mentioning the Ring, and their capture by Saruman's Orcs. They find that they have a friend in common—Gandalf—as well as an enemy—Saruman, who has been pillaging the forest.

Through calm courage, kindness, and good sense, Merry and Pippin make friends with Treebeard, and so gain a powerful ally for their cause. After reflection, Treebeard calls a convocation of the other Ents, and the huge creatures decide to attack Saruman's tower at Isengard, and put a stop to the wizard's evildoing. The Ents march, Merry and Pippin perched high up on Treebeard's shoulders, and at night hobbits and Ents avenge the wrongs they have suffered at the hands of Saruman and his servants. By the time Gandalf and others of the fellowship arrive with the Riders of Rohan to fight Saruman, Isengard is already destroyed, the battle won.

Merry and Pippin, then, play an important part in the first victory over the forces of darkness, and they accomplish it through friendship, which is the essence of international diplomacy. Again, as Elrond declared, small hands turn the wheels of power and accomplish great deeds.

Merry and Pippin prove their valor, and also mark the hour of the Shire-folk officially, with an addition to Treebeard's formal, poetic lists of living creatures. To his long, descriptive verses, among Man, Ents, Dwarves, and Elves— the free peoples—Treebeard adds "the Hobbit children, the laughing-folk, the little people," and so the child-race of Middle-earth leaves behind obscurity, and enters history.

IN the magic kingdom of Middle-earth, your child discovers that great historical events are sometimes the results of very small, private actions, and that courage is sometimes a matter of remaining calm in difficult circumstances. When public life is dramatized to reveal this truth, your child understands that her life isn't so very different from the lives of adults. In the same way, Frodo, Sam, Merry, and Pippin realize that they haven't become other people now that they are out in the world. They are simply expressing what has always been inside them, waiting for a challenge.

The first great danger brought about by the evil power of the Ring is the kind of trouble every child can understand, and most have experienced in some form. Determined to use the Ring himself, Boromir tries to talk Frodo into lending it to him. When this fails, the man lurches forward and tries to seize the Ring from Frodo, just as one child might try to grab a toy from another. Terrified by the sudden change that has come over Boromir, Frodo jumps back just in time, slips on the Ring, and invisibly escapes. Behind him, Boromir falls to the ground, dazed, and is immediately ashamed of himself.

Boromir doesn't know what came over him, but the perceptive Frodo does. The hobbit doesn't blame Boromir for wanting the Ring—that is, after all, part of its evil power— but to ignore the incident would be dangerous. Now Frodo must decide by himself what he must do for the safety of all Middle-earth, and he must set about it at once.

The wisest of the elves, Elrond, ordained that the burden of the Ring should be undertaken in fellowship, but Elrond isn't here now, just when the fellowship is in danger of breaking apart. Gandalf, too, is gone, and believed dead. Like a child away from his parents for the first time, Frodo has to assess the situation on his own, trying not to be frightened, so he can decide how to act.

It is then that Frodo realizes he must take the Ring to Mordor by himself. He is on his way when Sam finds him and begs to go along with him. Again deciding for himself, Frodo accepts Sam's company. Elrond's wisdom will be Frodo's guide when it confirms what Frodo himself feels is right. Love and loyalty may be the only powers great enough to stand against the evil of the Ring.

When the fellowship breaks apart, the plot divides into two separate yet related stories, both with childlike hobbits at their center. Frodo and Sam set out for Mount Doom, while Merry and Pippin, with the rest of the company, are headed toward the battles of Isengard, Minas Tirith, and the last great combat at the Gates of Mordor.

One hobbit group is on its own, alone in the realm of Sauron, small and defenseless, yet about to accomplish the undoing of the powers of darkness. The other hobbits are going to be participants as well as witnesses to history, in the clash of great armies and the death of kings. But the magic kingdom of Middle-earth offers both adventures—Frodo's lonely spiritual journey and Merry and Pippin's royal martial progress—as closely related and equally important, fitting challenges for child-heroes.

AS your child follows the story of Merry and Pippin, he sees these hobbits grow in confidence, experience, and even stature, as they face the challenges of a world plunged into war. When Aragorn, Legolas, Gimli, and Gandalf—who has been restored to life—arrive at Isengard and find Merry and Pippin calm and good-humored among the ruins of the enemy's stronghold, they remark how grown the hobbits seem. Merry and Pippin have indeed "grown" literally taller as the result of drinking Entish water.

But they have also grown in the ways of the world, a fact

their friends acknowledge with eager questions about the time the hobbits spent among the mysterious, reclusive Ents. What are the Ents like, the rest of the travelers want to know. In his reply, Pippin shows that he has grown in wisdom. About Ents, he says, "well the Ents are all different, for one thing," just as all individuals are, no matter where you find them.

With the onset of war, Pippin goes with Gandalf to the fortress city of Minas Tirith in Gondor and Merry goes with Aragorn, Legolas, and Gimli to Rohan, to prepare the two great powers to join in battle against the forces of the Dark Lord. Again, when the story divides, a hobbit appears in each part, a child-hero ready for action wherever we turn. Both Merry and Pippin have similar experiences in Rohan and in Gondor. Each of them, upon meeting the ruler, finds his heart touched with affection and respect, and spontane-ously—like Frodo at Rivendell—offers his services as a knight, an act of courage and courtesy that is received with the grace it deserves.

Merry and Pippin are sincere in their pledges of service to Théoden of Rohan and Denethor of Gondor, but when war breaks out they find that they've been left behind, the judg-ment being that they are too small to join in the great battle ahead. Still, the unfolding story of *The Lord of the Rings* has always affirmed the truth that no one is too small or too young for courageous action. In the midst of the epic strug-gle between good and evil at the gates of Minas Tirith, Merry and Pippin each find a way to play a heroic part.

Within the walled city, Pippin rescues Denethor's wounded son when the father, mad with despair, tries to kill himself and his son by climbing onto a funeral pyre with him. Outside, Merry has come to the battle with another warrior left behind by the forces of Rohan, the Lady Éowyn, and together they fight the winged Lord of the Nazgûl, who has killed Théoden of Rohan.

Éowyn, disguised as a young man, raises her sword against her uncle's killer. Laughing grimly, the Lord of the Nazgûl boasts, "No living man may hinder me!" But Éowyn is a woman, and Merry is one of the "hobbit-children," and so between them they destroy Sauron's dread warlord. Again, small hands are turning the wheels of history.

YOUR own child shares in the victory of good over evil at the Battle of Minas Tirith, when the hobbits prove themselves as worthy in war as they were in diplomacy. And once more, heroism is expressed not in arrogance or bravado, but in confidence and decisive action.

Earlier, when Pippin first arrived in Minas Tirith, the young hobbit reveals what is so impressive about all the hobbits, the child-heroes of this magic kingdom. After he has been received into the Steward's service, Pippin is escorted through the city by the guard Beregond. Beregond admits thinking at first that Pippin was a child of nine. After talking with the hobbit about his travels, the guard declares that Pippin has seen and experienced more than most adults, and he asks his new friend's pardon if he treated him in a patronizing way.

With grace and dignity, Pippin insists there is no need for concern. Unabashed, the hobbit concedes, "I am still little more than a boy in the reckoning of my own people, and it will be four years yet before I 'come of age,' as we say in the Shire."

Then, with interest, Pippin turns the conversation away from himself, and to the subject of Minas Tirith, asking Beregond enthusiastically to tell him about the city. Courtesy, self-esteem, and confidence characterize this view of Pippin, an image that casts a beautiful and generous reflection on your own child as well.

WHEN the small figures of Merry and Pippin shine in the large tapestry of battle, your child imaginatively shares in their victory. The young hobbits—the children of Middle-earth—

prove their worth by equaling the leaders in wisdom, courage, and courtesy in a time of crisis. It is a triumph children especially relish, and the magic kingdom of Middle-earth bestows its laurels with joy and pride.

At the same time, in the other sphere of action, Frodo and Sam are also proving themselves, but they are facing their challenge alone, with no one else nearby for comparison. Yet their journey is far more treacherous, and ultimately more crucial, to the fate of Middle-earth than the great battles of Isengard and Minas Tirith. At the Day of Doom, all the armies of the free peoples will depend on Frodo and Sam for their deliverance.

For Frodo and Sam, heroism is not glory in battle, but endurance in the desolate, dangerous Land of Shadows. As they make their way toward Mordor, the very source of evil in Middle-earth, in constant peril of discovery by the Dark Lord and his servants, they suffer hunger and thirst. They despair of completing their quest. Lonely, powerless, unbearably weary, they continue on their way.

Feeling terribly small in the middle of a frightening world, when all you can do is to endure and to hope, is an experience all children can understand. But this, too, is heroic action.

On their lonely, dangerous journey, Frodo and Sam encounter Sméagol, or Gollum, the murderous goblin who held the Ring before Bilbo. Still consumed with desire for his "Precious," as Sméagol calls the Ring, he has tracked Frodo and Sam for days, and is prepared to kill the "nasty hobbitses" for the prize.

At one time, upon hearing of Bilbo's meeting with the ghastly creature, Frodo had commented that it was a pity his uncle hadn't killed Sméagol when he had the chance. Gandalf sternly reproved Frodo, declaring that, in fact, "it was pity stayed his hand," and predicted that Bilbo's sparing of Sméagol would prove to be fortuitous as well as merciful. Who knows, Gandalf then mused; Sméagol may yet play a part in saving Middle-earth.

With Gandalf's wisdom suddenly brought to his memory,

and the sight of Sméagol, a shriveled, wasted slave of the Dark Lord, before him, Frodo pities the miserable goblin, and lets him live. Almost crushed himself by the burden of the Ring, Frodo feels genuine sympathy for a creature who has also felt the weight and dread might of its power. In return for his life, Sméagol leads Frodo and Sam into Mordor, although he does not know their purpose in going there.

The first result of Frodo's pity jeopardizes the quest, and almost seems to disprove Gandalf's prophecy about Sméagol. Although grateful to Frodo, the goblin cannot resist the temptation to seize the Ring for himself, and so he leads the hobbits into a trap, the lair of Shelob, a giant spider.

The monster attacks Frodo, apparently killing him, as Sméagol flees. Pity has endangered Frodo, but love rescues him. At last given an opportunity to prove himself, Sam drives Shelob back with Sting, Frodo's magic sword, and a vial of elven water that casts a miraculous light into the dark lair. Believing his beloved master dead, Sam takes the Ring and prepares to go on alone, as Frodo would have wished.

Sam's term as Ringbearer is short but crucial. Making himself invisible by slipping on the Ring, Sam learns from the Orc guards that Shelob paralyzes her prey before gorging on it. Frodo is not dead, but paralyzed.

Still invisible, Sam follows the Orcs as they take Frodo to their fortress, and he rescues his master from their dungeon. Once outside the fortress, Sam gives the Ring back to Frodo, and so becomes only the second Ringbearer in history to give it up willingly. All his actions, from the unsheathing of Sting to the return of the Ring, are heroic expressions of friendship and love, the heart's power, as Elrond acknowledged when he permitted Sam to accompany Frodo on the journey.

AT last they reach Mount Doom, the place where Frodo must throw the Ring into the consuming fire that Sauron used in creating it. All the sacrifices and the dangers they have endured have been to bring them to this moment on the edge of the Cracks of Doom. The fate of Middle-earth depends upon their success in bringing the Ring to this mountain. Once the Ring is returned to the ancient fire, the power of the Dark Lord will be destroyed, and a new world born.

At this crucial moment, Frodo suffers a paralysis of the will—he can't cast the Ring into the fires of Mount Doom. Succumbing to its evil power, Frodo seizes the Ring and cries that it is his, and he will not destroy it.

Suddenly, as if called by a magic incantation, Sméagol appears and fights Frodo for "the Precious." In a fierce struggle, literally on the edge of Doom, they wrestle, Frodo invisible because he is wearing the Ring. Sméagol savagely bites Frodo's finger and gains the Ring. The goblin dances for joy, waving the trophy wildly, then loses his balance and falls with the Ring into the fire of Mount Doom. And so, as Gandalf predicted, Sméagol did have a part to play in the destruction of the Ring, and Middle-earth is saved because of Frodo's pity for the wretched creature.

When the Ring falls into the fire, Sauron's evil power immediately dissolves. All of Mordor shakes, towers crumble, the Nazgûl evaporate. At the Gate of Mordor, where the armies of the free peoples and the Dark Lord's hosts are locked in mortal combat, Aragorn, in command, sees the enemy scatter before him, while a black cloud rises and is blown away. All these marvels, Gandalf announces, are proof that the Ringbearer has fulfilled the quest. It is the end of Mordor, and the beginning of a new Middle-earth.

A MAGIC kingdom imparts truth through imagination, raising up its child-hero to affirm your own child's goodness and strength. Its story teaches quite simply that when a child stands up for what is right, whether at a Mad Tea Party or in the shadow of Doom, that courage makes a difference, and can even save the world.

The child-heroes of The Lord of the Rings save their world through courage, love, and cooperation—qualities Frodo, Sam, Merry, and Pippin find were always within them. But it is only when they answer the call to leave the world they know and to face new challenges in the magic kingdom that their strength is truly expressed. In finding a new world, they find themselves, and win their crowns.

Frodo is the chief of the child-heroes, and, appropriately, he gains an immortality that is more than just metaphorical. In honor of his heroism, Aragorn's elven bride, Arwen, gives Frodo her place in the boat that will take her people over the far western seas. There Frodo will be healed of his terrible wounds and relieved of the pain inflicted by the burden of the Ring. And he will live forever.

Merry and Pippin return to the Shire as Bilbo once did, taller, bolder, and full of exciting stories. Their neighbors consider them warriors and adventurers now, rather than just young mischief-makers, and accord them honor and respect.

Part of this change towards the hobbits arises from the heroism they all show when they first arrive home and find that the Shire has been taken over by a "Sharkey" and his bullying henchmen. Stores have been plundered, trees cut down, and the town frightened into a state of dumb terror, until the four returning heroes find this "Sharkey" holed up in Bilbo's own Bag End, and recognize him as Saruman, the evil wizard who escaped the destruction of Isengard.

The hobbits left their home as Mole left Mole End, because a wider world was calling, and now they must win it back as Toad and his friends win back Toad Hall from the invading weasels. Whether at Toad Hall or Isengard or Bag End, a bully is a bully, and the only way to stand against a tyrant is to show him that the game is up—the same lesson that Alice teaches the Queen of Hearts and Peter Pan teaches Captain Hook.

Calmly and firmly, they confront the miserable wizard and his assistant, and order them out of the Shire. Desperate, Saruman tries to stab Frodo, but fails. Even then Frodo's heroic restraint holds, and out of pity the hobbit spares his life. As the two wretches leave, the assistant, angered by years of abuse, cuts his master's throat, and is killed by the arrows of Sam, Merry, and Pippin.

After the "scouring" of the Shire, there are still more heroic deeds to accomplish. Sam, as Frodo's heir, the master of Bag End, celebrates victory by calling the Shire back into the fullness of life. In the year after the war's end, Sam, a gifted gardener, plants new trees and flowers everywhere, and ensures their bounty with elven dust, a gift from the elven queen Galadriel.

The effect of Sam's love and Galadriel's magic is a Shire more verdant, fruitful, and beautiful than anyone can remember. The new growth is a symbol of triumph among the hobbits, and Sam becomes the figurative father of Hobbiton, as well as the father of his own growing family.

In a story as big as a world, planting and caring for trees and flowers symbolizes the beginning of a better life, and even seems, magically, to make it happen. An unhappy but determined child in a secret garden sets about weeding, and finds she feels less sullen and more friendly. The hero of a child-race tucks seeds in the earth with grains of blessed dust, and as the world grows rich and verdant, presides happily over his family and his town. It is a drama of growth in the truest sense, and at the center of the magic kingdom— whether a small English garden or a vast and mighty world— stands a child-hero who is, through the power of imagination, your own child.

IN the landscape of childhood imagination, your child will grow in courage, hope, resourcefulness, and responsibility, to become a hero of adventure and challenges, the ruler of the magic kingdom. At the end of their first adventure in Narnia, in *The Lion, the Witch and the Wardrobe,* Peter, Susan, Edmund, and Lucy ride on a royal hunt, to capture the White Stag said to grant wishes. They are kings and queens of Narnia, and have reigned for many years by that world's time, and so they spur their horses on through the forest with daring and grace.

The stag disappears in a thicket, and the four dismount to

follow. There they see something strange and dark, a post with a lantern that appears to be rising up from the ground directly before them. Lucy tells the others she has a strange feeling that if they pass the post and lantern, they will find great adventure and changes.

It is a challenge no king or queen of Narnia can in honor refuse. They all make for the strange object, wondering what lies beyond it, yet feeling prepared for whatever it may be. When they draw closer, they suddenly realize what it is—the lamppost—and then the branches around them become a jumble of hangers and coats. Before they know it, they are stepping out of the wardrobe and are back in England, just minutes after they left.

This isn't a trick or a disappointment. The magic kingdom, in returning its rulers to the life of the real world, has granted their wish, despite the stag's escape. Great adventure and changes do await the children—and your own child—in this world, after the closing of the wardrobe and the closing of the book. The biggest challenge is still to come. It's growing up.

CHAPTER SEVEN

Over the Rainbow
—and Beyond

WE leave the magic kingdom, but it never leaves us. In fact, it's just when we think we've left childhood behind us that we discover it all over again with our children. Then we open a favorite book from our past and the landscape of imagination stretches before us again, just as we remembered, closer than we thought.

The classic stories of the magic kingdom carried us forward through imagination, helping us to envision an older, abler version of ourselves, confident and triumphant in a different world. And because the purpose of the fantasy is growth rather than escape, the child-hero's victory comes from self-expression—Alice's common sense, Christopher Robin's love for his Forest friends, Mole's desire to be helpful. All these characters, we see, grow to heroism not by changing into someone else, but by accepting changes outside, while remaining essentially themselves inside. The details of life and work will change, these stories illustrate, but you will always be you.

In childhood, the stories of the magic kingdom carried us forward. Now, with our own children, they can carry us back in imagination, to the time we first heard them read, or read them ourselves. So when you open a favorite book to read with your child, be ready for the delight and excitement you felt the first time you tumbled down the rabbit-hole with Alice, found your way through the wardrobe with Lucy, or flew out the nursery window with Wendy. In reading again the stories you loved as a child, you'll find within you that enduring legacy of imagination, and be able to share it in love with your own child, in preparation for a life of growth and of challenge.

WHEN I was four, I was Peter Pan. In my imagination, I flew effortlessly all around my room, inspired by the Golden Book edition of Barrie's story, which I'd memorized, and Mary Martin's performance on television. When I'd done with swooping and gliding within four walls, I would fly out the window and over the housetops. Second to the right, and straight on till morning.

Of course, I understood I couldn't *really* fly. I had the beautiful thoughts, but no fairy dust. But if I didn't have the fairy dust, I did have a hat and slippers made of green construction paper. With these, I felt I not only *was* Peter Pan, but that everyone who saw me would know it. I was so happy and proud, I wore my Peter Pan outfit everywhere, even, on one occasion, on a shopping trip downtown to Saks Fifth Avenue.

I don't remember why I decided to wear the Peter Pan hat and slippers, which fit over my shoes, or what kind of interest my appearance created in the store that day. More than likely, I'd thought my costume was appropriate, since Saks Fifth Avenue was famous for its window exhibit every Christmas featuring animated puppets, usually in scenes from classic children's books. So perhaps this was my way of joining in the tradition.

Just a few years ago, I took my daughter Franny to Saks to see the Christmas display. It was a Saturday morning, and there was, as usual, quite a crowd slowly making its way past the window on Fifth Avenue. Mothers and fathers lifted their babies from strollers, while older children stood on the tips of their snow boots to gaze at the animated scene.

Franny and I moved patiently with the crowd until we reached the window. What we found on the other side of the glass was a miniature magic kingdom, a scene with the characters from *The Lion, the Witch and the Wardrobe*. All the children around us were wide-eyed, and every parent pointed as Aslan, the Lion, crowned Peter the High King of Narnia, ruler of the magic kingdom. Here, in the middle of the city, was a magical vision of childhood we all could share.

*   *   *

AS you and your child read books together, inevitably it makes both of you more conscious of the world and its surprises. So it's easy to imagine the parents and children who were taking their customary stroll through London's Kensington Gardens on the May morning in 1912 when they discovered something amazing—the figure of Peter Pan on a pedestal, where yesterday there had been nothing at all.

Sculpted by Sir George Frampton, by arrangement with J. M. Barrie himself, the statue had been erected overnight, secretly, to make it seem as if Peter Pan had suddenly appeared in the park by magic one spring morning. It was an inspired idea, and just the sort of surprise to make the boy who wouldn't grow up—and all his friends—crow with delight.

Barrie loved Kensington Gardens, because it was the place where he had spent time with his friends the Llewelyn-Davies boys, walking his Newfoundland dog, who was the inspiration for Nana. They had played here often, and it was here that they first talked about Peter Pan, making up stories that they played out for years.

In tribute to the park, Barrie had made Kensington Gardens the birthplace of Peter Pan. Another author might have been better pleased with a quiet, formal plaque noting the significance of the place, but Barrie preferred a statue of the character, and he chose one of the Llewelyn-Davies brothers, Michael, to be the sculptor's model for Peter.

Instead of a grown-up tribute to impress other grown-ups, Barrie put the statue of Peter Pan in the magical setting where Peter first came to our world. It is a monument to a fantasy created by a few children and one child at heart, shared first by them, and now by all of us, in childhood imagination, in our dreams of freedom, and in our play.

To create in physical space—a park—what is held in the imagination expresses a connection, a common bond among us. The statue of Peter Pan delights us because we recognize in it the symbol of a character we love. Seeing it displayed in a public park reminds us that our enjoyment is shared by many others, in a community of imagination.

WITH the same magical effect as Peter Pan in Kensington Gardens, Alice is seated on a giant mushroom in the middle of New York's Central Park. The statue, showing Alice with the White Rabbit and the Mad Hatter on either side and the Cheshire Cat peering at us over her shoulder, attracts parents and children all year round, and seems an invitation to play and to imagine. I know, because as a child and as an adult, I've never seen Alice in Central Park without wanting to read her book again as soon as I got home.

Donated in 1959 by the publisher George T. Delacorte, the statue honors the memory of his wife Margarita, who read *Alice's Adventures in Wonderland* to their six children. In the last years of his life, Delacorte visited the statue often, and would watch happily at a distance while children scrambled around and climbed on the Wonderland setting, trying to get a close look at Alice's face, reaching up toward her outstretched hand.

When you see the happiness and the joyful play that come from your child's imaginative encounter with Alice or Peter Pan or any of the child-heroes of the magic kingdom, you understand how important and powerful an experience it can be. The bravery, the common sense, the freedom of the child-hero call to your child to play, and, in playing, to create a self that will withstand any challenge with courage, wit, and grace, as Alice herself does.

WHEN I was a child, I loved *Alice's Adventures in Wonderland* and *The Wonderful Wizard of Oz,* and I took delight in remembering the smallest details of the stories, and all the poems and songs. It seemed strange, then, that sometimes I mixed up the names of my favorite characters, Alice and Dorothy. When I couldn't remember the name of the girl who goes to Oz, "Alice" invariably popped into my mind.

It was as if Alice and Dorothy were the same character, and their names were different words for the same identity. A child named Alice, a child named Dorothy, a little bored by her surroundings, suddenly finds herself in another world—a dazzling, strange place, a magic kingdom she has never seen or dreamed of until now.

As beautiful as it is, this world challenges the girl, testing her courage, wisdom, and sympathy, compelling her to stand up for herself in ways she hasn't before. She faces all the challenges, overcomes the power of evil, sees through absurdity, and wins the crown. Only after she has triumphed in the magic kingdom does she find the way home. And then, she finds, her home isn't boring at all.

The adventures of Alice and the adventures of Dorothy are different, but the same. Both are stories of the magic kingdom, celebrating a child's strength and goodness, inviting your child to triumph in imagination with the heroine as she stands up for what she knows is right. In a real sense, the two characters are the same, too. Alice is the quintessential ruler of the magic kingdom, and Dorothy is the twentieth-century American Alice.

AFTER the great popular success of *The Wonderful Wizard of Oz*, published in 1900, Lyman Frank Baum was sometimes known as the Royal Historian of that magic kingdom. It was as if Oz existed in fact—a magical place located on the map, with a real history that Baum had merely recorded rather than invented.

As a child, living in a large, comfortable house in Syracuse, New York, Baum enjoyed reading fairy tales, particularly those of Hans Christian Andersen. He also loved working with his own printing press and dreaming up plays to produce. The Baum family's wealth, from the Pennsylvania oil fields, gave the boy the freedom and resources to experiment with all his hobbies, and his precarious health—a heart condition at age twelve—was another probable inducement for his parents' indulgence of their son's interests.

By his late twenties, Baum had worked as an actor, playwright, theatre manager, salesman, and newspaper editor. He had also written two books, one on raising chickens, the other on decorating shop windows. He had been more or less successful in all his occupations, but somehow had never managed to develop a steady income, or, just as important, a sense of professional direction.

In 1897, at the age of forty-one, Baum started what would be his real career. He began writing down the stories he'd told his sons—what he thought of as modern fairy tales—and he found a publisher. In Baum's first book for children, *Mother Goose in Prose,* he presented the stories of traditional English nursery rhymes with modern American children in mind. In *Father Goose, His Book,* two years later, Baum himself wrote the nursery rhymes, again to please the American children of his own time. With illustrations by W. W. Denslow, the attractive volume was the best-selling children's book of the year.

The enormous success of *Father Goose* solved Baum's problem of income and gave him a professional identity. He was a writer of children's books, in great demand by publishers, and he had enough ideas to keep him writing for quite some time.

In his children's stories, Baum wanted to write as imaginatively as Andersen, but in a modern voice. Lewis Carroll had done this in the *Alice* books, which Baum greatly admired, and he commented that the reason children love Alice more than any fairy princess of Andersen's is that Alice is a real child with whom they can sympathize.

Lewis Carroll, in Baum's view, had invented a new kind of fairy tale for modern children. What Carroll had done in England, Baum was determined to accomplish in America. The magic kingdom was going to cross the ocean and take root in the New World.

Baum tried his experiment in a collection of stories he titled, significantly, *A New Wonderland.* But, like Kenneth

Grahame, Baum had some difficulty getting his magic kingdom into focus at first. Baum's "Phuniland," like Grahame's "Golden City," is a riot of root-beer rivers and candy that grows on bushes, all sweets and no substance.

In the same year, 1900, Baum's *The Wonderful Wizard of Oz* also featured a magic land of imagination. At first, Baum proposed as its title *The Emerald City*. When the publisher objected, he suggested *The Fairyland of Oz*. Finally, the book was published under the title *The Wonderful Wizard of Oz*, and with it Baum achieved his goal of bringing the modern fairy tale—the magic kingdom—to American children, and giving them their own Alice, an American girl to sympathize with and to cheer.

IN a short note at the beginning of *The Wonderful Wizard of Oz*, Baum explained his new kind of fairy tale, which he called a "wonder tale." The story of Oz that follows celebrates the glories of fantasy rather than its terrors, emphasizing growth and strength, the natural goodness of children, and new imaginative possibilities, instead of supernatural enchantment and entrapment. Of course, Baum includes dangers and wicked witches in his story of Oz, but they are there to be conquered by Dorothy.

Baum wanted his new kind of children's story, his "wonder tale," to emphasize the glory and excitement of fairy tales without the terrors traditionally included in them. The greatest power in Oz, as in all magic kingdoms, is at a child's command. When the magic arrives, it doesn't take the form of an ancient genie in a bottle, but a girl in a cyclone.

Dorothy Gale's power is part of her character—even her name tells us that—and with it she destroys evil without even meaning to. Just by arriving in Oz, Dorothy kills the wicked Witch of the East, and just by stepping into the Witch's shoes, changes evil magic to good. All that is left is for Dorothy to become conscious of what she has done, and what she is capable of doing.

For Dorothy, as for your own child, the challenges of Oz

are the challenges of the magic kingdom, and its rewards honor the courage, wisdom, and love expressed spontaneously by its child-hero. And like Alice, Dorothy isn't a girl who is just hoping to be rescued. She is destined to rule.

JUST as the child-hero of a magic kingdom suddenly finds herself on the threshold of a different world without ever meaning to travel there, a writer one day sees something intriguing, a glimmer of an idea, and follows it into the landscape of imagination. When the story is placed in a child's hands, the map that appears at the front of the book shows a land that has revealed itself to the writer, for a magic kingdom isn't so much created as discovered, usually when least expected.

It's said that while Baum was telling a story one evening, he happened to glance at the file cabinet in the corner of the room. Noticing the label on the bottom drawer, O–Z, Baum included the letters in his narrative as the name of a special place, the magical land of Oz.

Whether or not this actually happened isn't certain, but it is a story with its own psychological truth. What Baum saw that evening anyone could see, but only he could find a meaning in it that would open the eyes of children and their parents to the wonder of imagination, in the Land of Oz.

THE popularity of Baum's *The Wizard of Oz,* its title, like *Alice's Adventures in Wonderland,* soon shortened by familiarity, led to a film production of the story. But the first film about Dorothy and Oz wasn't the musical we know best. The first production was Baum's own *Fairylogues and Radio Plays,* an ambitious multimedia show that premiered in Chicago in 1908 and toured the country.

The author himself appeared onstage, dressed, the newspapers noted, in an elegant white suit. After an introductory speech, Baum disappeared behind a large screen where, suddenly, he reappeared on film with his Oz characters—Dorothy, the Wizard, the Scarecrow, and the rest—and assisted them as they stepped out of a large book. Scenes from Baum's books, *The Wonderful Wizard of Oz, The Marvelous Land of Oz,* and *Ozma of Oz,* were dramatized on film, with an orchestra, also on stage, providing the music. In between the scenes, to rest the audience's eyes, Baum explained, there were still slides of the characters shown on the screen.

The show was a critical and popular success, but when Baum realized how much money he was losing through the expense of the production, he had to close the tour. Yet in its ambitious blending of film, music, and live action, *Fairylogues and Radio Plays* made possible the movie and cartoon adaptations of classic books that we loved as children and you and your child enjoy today. The man in the white suit who helped Dorothy to leap from the pages of a book and into action demonstrated for his audience the next possibility for the magic kingdom.

IT seems, somehow, as if there must always have been an Oz. The story of Dorothy Gale and her adventures in Oz is so much a part of our culture now that you may find it difficult to pinpoint exactly when your child—or you—became familiar with it. The characters, phrases, and images of Dorothy's story, like Alice's, have long since spilled over into daily life, so that we talk of a Cowardly Lion or a Mad Hatter confident that we'll be understood.

When Franny was four, I took her to see *The Wizard of Oz* in a movie theatre. The lights went down and the screen was suddenly lit up with the title, and I felt the same excitement as when we opened a book together. In the theatre with us were dozens of other parents and children, all of us sharing together a delight that we'd each enjoyed in our own homes.

After the opening credits, a few sentences about the story by L. Frank Baum appeared, and I could hear many hushed voices of adults reading in whispers to the children beside them, just as I was, that this film was dedicated to those who had been true to the story, and to the young in heart.

"It's dedicated to me," Franny whispered back in delight, and then settled herself to watch.

We love *The Wizard of Oz* because the film plays with the story as a child does when pretending to be Dorothy, or Alice, or Christopher Robin. Like a child, the movie seems to know what is and is not essential; what can be changed for convenience and fun and what should remain the same.

When she was very young, we'd given Franny a paper-doll theatre of *The Wizard of Oz,* and watched with pride as she moved and manipulated the dolls and the elements of the story in varying ways, emphasizing what were for her the most interesting parts, while skipping over or condensing others. The film follows the same free play, by substituting the more cinematic ruby slippers for the silver shoes of the book, and by folding all the kingships won by the Cowardly Lion, the Scarecrow, and the Tin Woodman into the single throne of Oz and the comic song of the Cowardly Lion, "If I Were King of the Forest."

In Baum's particularly American story of the magic kingdom, the child-hero herself isn't literally crowned, but she helps her friends to rise to kingship. Dorothy has become the queen of their hearts without the encumbrance of a crown. The film celebrates Dorothy's generous and noble nature even more by doubling her new, magical friends in Oz with her old friends from the Kansas farm.

In her dream of Oz, Dorothy helps to make the dreams of her farm friends come true. This adventure—another version of Christopher Robin's responsibility for his friends in the Forest—makes Dorothy realize that the land of freedom and magic she longed to find "over the rainbow" is actually in her own backyard, and within herself.

DOROTHY enters her magic kingdom by opening a door, as if the Land of Oz really is her backyard. In the movie, her passage from our world into this place over the rainbow is accomplished through the most famous special effect in film history, elegant in its simplicity. Dorothy, in her black-and-white Kansas farmhouse, opens the door to reveal outside Oz's world of radiant colors.

Like Mole running from his dusty, dim hole and suddenly overcome by his first vision of the River Bank, verdant and beautiful, Dorothy sees a world full of life, color, and possibility. This is indeed a magic kingdom, not only because it is a realm of imagination and challenge, but because when Dorothy steps into the landscape, we see her differently, too. She is no longer the black-and-white figure against a gray background, but a vibrant girl on the threshold of womanhood in a magical land. Now we see Dorothy isn't just a farm girl, but a girl who will be queen.

But Dorothy doesn't see herself and her own strength and beauty as we do. Again and again she expresses her goodness and power impulsively, doing what's right without even thinking about it. Early in the movie, when Toto is in danger of being killed, Dorothy immediately runs away to save him, and when she understands that her leaving will grieve her aunt and uncle, she returns home just as impulsively. And it is this combination of actions—with love as the motivation—that brings Dorothy back to her house too late for shelter in the storm cellar, and just in time for a journey to Oz.

DOROTHY's challenge in the magic kingdom of Oz is not to *become* good, but to become conscious of the goodness she has always expressed naturally. Dorothy is much more powerful than she thinks. She just needs an experience that will allow her to prove it to herself. Once she discovers what she is capable of in Oz, she'll be able to begin the greatest adventure of all, the one she thinks requires the help of a wizard—going home.

On the yellow brick road, Dorothy meets three characters who are also unconscious of their strengths, just as she is. We see that the three actually have the intelligence, heart, and courage they long for. If the Scarecrow knows how to free himself from the pole and can use reverse psychology to get apples from talking trees, then obviously he must have a brain. The kind and sentimental Tin Woodman shows us with every word and action that he has a heart, just as the Cowardly Lion makes it clear that he has courage enough to face any enemy of Dorothy's.

In a sense, the Scarecrow, the Tin Woodman, and the Cowardly Lion represent Dorothy as well as being characters themselves. They are another way of making the point that Dorothy already has within her the power to link the worlds of fantasy and reality—Oz and Kansas—and that she doesn't need a wizard to find her way home.

In fact, it is Dorothy herself who calls forth the heroic qualities in her friends, because she provides them with the opportunity to prove themselves through supporting, advising, and even rescuing her. In helping her friends to realize their gifts, she discovers her own, and she is revealed in the magic kingdom of Oz to be not only the child-hero but the very culmination of its tradition.

But before Dorothy is able to see herself as she really is— brave, resourceful, a force for good—she must conquer the other evil in the Land of Oz, the wicked Witch of the West. In the film, the Witch is melted when the girl impulsively throws a bucket of water on her while trying to save the Scarecrow from burning. In Baum's book, she dumps the bucket of water on the Witch deliberately, in anger, but without knowing the effect this will have. In both scenes, the Wicked Witch melts away, in shocked amazement at Dorothy's power. The girl, too, is astounded by what she has done, never intending to kill the Witch at all. Still, she has saved the Land of Oz from evil forever, by accident.

But there are no accidents in the magic kingdom. The child-hero answers the challenge and triumphs, not because of what she does, but because of what she *is*—generous, intelligent, courageous. Whether in anger or in love, Dorothy always acts heroically, like Peter Pan, showing "good form without knowing it" in following her impulses. Such a child has it in her power to rule all of Oz, if she chooses. But she is the only one who doesn't realize it.

OF course, Dorothy is very powerful, but doesn't know it. And the Wizard she looks to for help is powerless, but nobody knows it except for him. He is revealed in the end as a virtual prisoner in his own palace, hiding behind disguises and subterfuge, and manipulating signs and symbols to keep his subjects in awe and at bay.

At their first meeting, Oz tells Dorothy and her friends that if they kill the Wicked Witch of the West he will give the Scarecrow brains, the Tin Woodman a heart, and the Lion courage, and send Dorothy home to Kansas. He presents this requirement as a test of their worthiness, but of course it's a hoax. Oz can't grant their wishes any more than he can destroy the Witch. It is Dorothy who holds the real power to save the Land of Oz from evil. It's the child-hero, not the Wizard, who is the true ruler of this magic kingdom.

Oz is a humbug, he admits when he is found out. He has no power to give what he has promised, but he can acknowledge with symbols the qualities of intelligence, courage, and love that Dorothy's friends already possess. Baum's Wizard bestows his gifts upon the Scarecrow, the Tin Woodman, and the Cowardly Lion as if the tokens actually were the virtues they represent, rather like a quack doctor at a county fair. In the movie, the Wizard explains to the three that they are already as wise, courageous, and loving as anyone could hope to be, and confers the diploma, the medal, and the clockwork heart in the style of a master of ceremonies.

The Wizard can assure Dorothy's friends of their heroic qualities by granting their wishes symbolically. Dorothy herself, however, is beyond the Wizard's authority and ability. He can't give Dorothy what she needs—the power to find her own way home—because her power is so much greater than his. The best he can do is offer her passage home to Kansas with him, in the way he came, by balloon.

Dorothy made her way to the Land of Oz in a cyclone, a force of nature, not an overgrown toy. The Wizard can play with tricks and carnival ploys, but Dorothy still must find the power within herself to return home. And, not surprisingly, her journey back begins as her journey there did. She misses the balloon, as she did the safety of the storm cellar, because she is looking for Toto.

When the Wizard's balloon—what she believes to be her last hope—is gone, Dorothy is in despair. Her friends try to comfort her, and in Baum's story they travel with her far to the South, to seek the advice of the Good Witch Glinda, returning the help that Dorothy gave them on the way to the Emerald City. In the movie, Glinda herself appears, the magic kingdom's alternative to the fairy godmother.

But instead of transporting Dorothy back to Kansas with a wave of her wand, Glinda explains to the girl that she needs no one's help, that she can return home by herself. All Dorothy has been lacking is belief in herself and the awareness that the greatest magical power in Oz is—literally—at her feet. Once Dorothy understands that all the wonder and magic she has thought of as being "over the rainbow" is really part of her, the shoes can take her home, where everyday life—*her* life—will be as full of adventure as the land in her dream.

"There's no place like home," Dorothy repeats in the film, her eyes closed. When she opens them, she finds herself at home, very much like Alice at the end of her adventures. Overjoyed, Dorothy tearfully promises never to leave again, and the movie ends with a repetition of the magical phrase, its nostalgia emphasized in the musical background, a quotation of the familiar song.

In Baum's book, however, Dorothy doesn't wake up, because her journey to Oz has been real. Yet she says something similar when she finds herself suddenly outside the Kansas farmhouse. Rushing to Aunt Em, she cries happily, "I'm so glad to be at home again!"

* * *

DOROTHY has helped her friends' wishes to come true, and she has learned the power of her own intelligence, courage, and compassion. She has left her friends as kings in Oz, crowning *them* instead of being crowned herself, and has returned to the everyday world confident that everything she dreamed can come true through her own power.

By the end, "Kansas" and "home" aren't words that mean boredom or frustration. Instead, they mean "Dorothy," the child-hero who ruled a magic kingdom and then left it for the bigger challenge of growing up. Now Dorothy feels at home with herself, secure, happy, and confident, knowing that everything she has been longing for was inside her all the time, and always will be.

Dorothy's self *is* her home now, and so when she says, "I'm glad to be home," it means "I'm glad to be me," just as all the child-heroes of the magic kingdom—and your own child, too—say "There's no place like home" and mean "There's no one like me."

WE want our children to feel confident and at home with themselves and in the world. The stories of the magic kingdom teach this sense of self-esteem by allowing your child to identify with the stories' characters through imagination, so that the success of the child-hero in the magic kingdom becomes your own child's promise of success in the real world. Despite challenges, despite changes, the stories assure children, you will still be you, even when you're all grown up.

Baum introduced the magic kingdom to America in *The Wizard of Oz,* and Dorothy, according to Baum's theory, would impress readers as being a "real child," yet equal in power and imagination to the heroine of a fairy tale. And, accordingly, the story of Dorothy and the magic kingdom of Oz came to be accepted—even assumed—as part of our cultural knowledge, very much like the traditional fairy tale. The story of the magic kingdom was on its way to being acknowledged as the true heir of the Brothers Grimm, Hans Christian Andersen, and Charles Perrault.

The embracing of the magic kingdom expresses itself most publicly in the animated films of Walt Disney, who brought the British classics to the screen in the same spirit as he adapted the stories of Snow White and Cinderella. With Disney's productions of the stories of Lewis Carroll and Milne, presented as the equals of the Grimms' or Andersen's, the children's classics reached their widest potential audience yet, and in the best company as well.

The magic kingdom came to the screen, and the stories of the child-hero in the magic kingdom are now the acknowledged favorites of a general—even a mass—audience. When the imaginary worlds and secret places we find in books and keep in our memories suddenly appear before us, we become conscious of the connection we share through the common landscape of childhood. Each of us still has a Wonderland of our own, but now we have one to share, too.

The Wizard of Oz had made clear the extraordinary power of film as a medium for a classic children's story, especially in bringing the imaginary and the real together on equal terms. In his adaptations of the stories of the magic kingdom, which are based on just such a meeting of fantasy and reality, Disney used cinematic techniques to underscore the magic meeting of two worlds, like the jump that Mary Poppins and her friends take into the chalk pavement picture, where they enjoy themselves in a fantasy landscape of animation.

There is also an affirmation of the connection between reality and imagination in our world in Disney's films. The *Winnie-the-Pooh* short features make this point in their opening, which begins in live action, with shots of a nursery where stuffed animals—Pooh, Piglet, and the rest—are prominently displayed. We next see them, and Christopher Robin, as cartoon characters in a picture we recognize as part of the map that serves as the endpapers to the *Pooh* books. The camera moves in closer and the characters start to move, fully animated now. As in Milne's original story, the nursery toys in the real world become the inspiration for the fantasy characters in the world represented in the map, and our imaginative engagement with those characters has brought them to life.

And the best-known path from reality to imagination is the opening theme of the other adaptations by Disney. Characteristically, at the beginning of a Disney film, we see a book opening, and then hear a narrator reading from the text, as if we in the audience were being read to from a favorite book. Then the camera reveals an illustration and draws closer to it, as though we were seeing it with our most acute child-sight. And once the illustration is so close that we seem almost to be in the picture ourselves, the characters start to move, as if our looking at them makes them magically come alive.

This characteristic opening recalls for us the time before we could read, when a story really did unfold in pictures, coming to life before our eyes. The films are an opportunity for older children and parents to recapture the immediacy and the excitement we felt as very young children, encountering for the first time a story of the child-hero in the magic kingdom.

AS parents, we know that the landscape of imagination exists in our shared vision of the magic and possibility of childhood and of life itself. The stories that taught us this truth still delight us and our children today. When we were growing up, the landscape of childhood imagination was also spoken of as a place you could actually visit—Disneyland. Like the statue of Peter Pan in Kensington Gardens, Alice in Central Park, or the windows of Saks Fifth Avenue at Christmas, Disneyland (and similar theme parks that followed) represent a concrete expression of belief that a child's imagination has its own reality; that shared fantasy is not only important, but must be publicly acknowledged and celebrated.

The theme park—a place built specifically to represent a

state of mind—is a uniquely American extension of the world of fantasy. It seems, at first, to be the opposite of an imaginative experience in reading or in watching a film, when we shut off immediate, everyday reality and enter the imaginary realm. But Disneyland provides its own special kind of imaginative experience, offering a direct, physical means of entering the land of imagination, literally through our senses, not despite them.

This is the road to fantasy we took as children, when we immersed ourselves in a story through play. In expressing an imaginative experience by pretending, we each made explicit—that is, public—our individual feelings about the story we were playing; asking, in fun, for confirmation of those feelings from others.

Disneyland promises both children and adults the opportunity to immerse themselves physically in certain stories. The success of the theme park is testimony to the power of returning in imagination to a child's view of stories, and our need, even as adults, to see and hear them accepted and approved by others.

As Disney saw it, his theme park would be a place where parents and children could participate actively in fantasy by entering a theatrical set representing the world of fantasy itself. Art direction, characters in costume, and special effects, everything was conceived to encourage children and adults to imagine that they have entered another world—the Magic Kingdom—and to experience it as directly and intensely as if it were real.

And, of course, it *is* real. Disneyland's distinctive quality is the power it has to persuade in its own way, by its own methods. In physical terms, Disneyland accomplishes the same imaginative goal of a classic book like *Alice in Wonderland* or a movie like *The Wizard of Oz*. It goes beyond the conventional suspension of disbelief and instead convinces you that there truly is a landscape of imagination, and that you're really there.

So to enter Disneyland, or any similar theme park, is to be

invited to imagine that the adventure of the child-hero in the magic kingdom is your adventure, that the imaginary has become real. Much is made in Disneyland of the stories we all know and hold in common, those fantasies that connect us with one another imaginatively and seem, somehow, to be connected themselves, in one small, marvelous landscape—"nicely crammed," as Peter Pan describes Neverland.

The Storybook Land Canal Boats of Disneyland play on this expectation. Gliding by a green countryside, we see a representation of the village of Alice in Wonderland, and then Kensington Gardens, where J. M. Barrie and his friends first played Peter Pan, and after that, stately Toad Hall. From a boat on a river that magically becomes the River, we can witness a literal landscape of imagination, with tales unfolding one after another, all together, just as we imagined.

DESPITE the elaborate effects and feats of engineering, a theme park is, after all, simply another way of playing with the elements of a favorite story, as a child does when building with blocks and moving figures around to represent action. And the popular appeal of Disneyland, and of all Disney fantasy, arises from our childlike desire to take these stories of the magic kingdom into our own hands and to shape them according to our own modern interests and needs. The same motivation continually creates new versions of children's classics—a faithful stage adaptation of *The Secret Garden* on Broadway, or a freewheeling film like Steven Spielberg's *Hook,* which carries the story of Peter Pan a generation beyond Barrie's ending.

We love the stories of the magic kingdom, and we want to make them new because we want to make them ours. The world of imagination we find in them offers the possibility of growing up without growing old, of becoming as wise as a wizard while retaining a child's heart. In reworking these tales of the child-hero, revising, even representing them in a different medium, we prove to ourselves not only that there really is a magic kingdom, but that we can find our way back there.

WHEN I read *Alice's Adventures in Wonderland* to Franny, I feel that I'm opening a beautiful world for my daughter while reentering it myself. The sound of the words, the lines of the drawings, the sight of Alice's pinafore, and the description of her fall down the rabbit-hole all vividly bring back the sense of my own childhood. It reminds me how long and how short a time it's been since I was the one looking intently at the letters, wondering how I could learn to change them magically into the story of a girl named Alice.

From the child-hero's perspective we can see the geography of the landscape of childhood imagination—remember Alice standing on the hill in the Looking-Glass World and gazing over the chessboard countryside? And in a larger context, our enduring perspective on reality and imagination—our shared sense of the world around us—is also the view we see when we identify with the child-hero.

The stories of the magic kingdom were received eagerly by their first audiences in nineteenth-century England because, like folktales, they explained life at a crucial moment in simple yet powerful terms. The world that waited ahead, a larger world of international responsibility and imperial power that England seemed to be entering as if drawn by magic, would be filled with challenge and even danger.

But the stories of Carroll, Grahame, Barrie, and Milne promised those first readers that a natural, childlike instinct for what is right could find and lead the way along the royal road to success. Despite the unforeseen circumstances, the complexity, and confusion that might lie ahead, there was always good form—Peter Pan's advantage—and good form was just what was needed to win the day.

When I was a child, growing up in the 1950s and 1960s, America assumed responsibility for power in a new, challenging world. The nineteenth-century stories of the magic kingdom returned, and they were received just as eagerly, this time at the movies as well as in books. Some of us met Christopher Robin and Alice in books and then were excited to see them in the movies, too. Others discovered the characters on screen, and later found them in books, where, through the secret language of reading, they magically came to life whenever they were called.

My generation was lucky to be growing up in that time, and the stories we loved live on in the part of each of us that remains always a child. And now that we are parents ourselves, it's natural that we want to pass along to our children the happiness we remember from the best times of our childhood.

Over the years of our own childhood, stories of the magic kingdom came to the screen—*The Wind in the Willows, Alice, Peter Pan, Mary Poppins, Winnie-the-Pooh,* and *The Jungle Book.* They appeared in a different medium, but their essence was preserved: A child suddenly finds himself in another world, a magic kingdom, where he will face the challenge of growth, will triumph through bravery, compassion, and intelligence to win the crown, and will then return to our world to find an even greater adventure in everyday life.

It is a vision of childhood that we still cherish today, and want to share with our own children. All our children, we believe, have within them heroic qualities—courage, intelligence, sympathy—even if they don't realize it, and need only a worthy challenge to prove it. The classics of the magic kingdom reveal this truth through imagination, and when our children identify with Alice, Christopher Robin, Mary Lennox, Dorothy, and other child-heroes, they will face the challenge of growth and become the rulers of a magic kingdom.

THESE classic stories endure despite the passage of time because they touch a chord in us, and in our children, that is timeless. All of us want to help our sons and daughters to realize their childhood imagination fully and consciously, and we want to rediscover our own childhood, too. You do this when you read your child a loved book, enjoy a classic movie together, or visit a theme park where both of you can play imaginatively. All of these experiences are worthwhile, a sharing of fantasy that can strengthen your love, bring you closer together, and encourage the awareness of childhood as a special time for exploring in imagination.

Now is the time for your child to imagine himself the ruler of a magic kingdom, the hero of his own childhood. In reading together books that open the door to a world of challenge and growth, in exploring together the landscape of imagination in all its forms, you help your child to make the journey of the child-hero, where he will prove his natural strength, intelligence, and love through his triumph in the magic kingdom. And the crown your child wins in imagination is the promise of a life touched by the best kind of magic, when the child-hero of the magic kingdom grows to be the hero of real life.

THE triumph of the child-hero in the magic kingdom is a story that touches something enduring in all of us. Now, as we share these best-loved stories with our own children, we want to give them the same happiness that we enjoyed while wandering in Christopher Robin's Forest, sharing the delight of Alice's coronation, and flying over Neverland with Peter and Wendy.

The classic children's books of the magic kingdom endure because they are loved, remembered, and happily passed on from parents to children. Besides the classic stories we've already talked about, here are some other books touched by the tradition of the magic kingdom that you'll want to share with your child. At the same time, as you explore and chart together the landscape of childhood imagination, your child will undoubtedly discover other stories of the magic kingdom on his own and share them with *you*.

BEMELMANS, LUDWIG
Bemelmans's *Madeline* is a classic, loved for its unforgettable heroine, the beautiful pictures of Paris, and the rhyming narration ("In an old house in Paris that was covered with vines/Lived twelve little girls in two straight lines"). Madeline is the smallest girl in her school, but she is also the bravest and the most fun. A child-hero, like Alice in Wonderland, she's a character who stays with you and makes you long to share her. Bemelmans's illustrations have a wonderful, fantasy quality to them, as if the Tuileries and Notre Dame are places in a magic kingdom. It is now published in a large

format, like the one in which, perhaps, you first met Madeline. Favorites among the sequels include *Madeline and the Bad Hat, Madeline's Rescue,* and *Madeline's Christmas.*

DAHL, ROALD
Dahl's wild fantasies show us children who take on greedy monsters—usually grown-ups—and triumph, as in *Danny, the Champion of the World* and *Matilda.* Dahl's best-known story, *Charlie and the Chocolate Factory,* is the tale of a child-hero who just needs a chance to prove himself, because, as Captain Hook would say, he has "good form without knowing it." Although so poor that a chocolate bar is a once-a-year birthday treat, Charlie Bucket finds one of Mr. Willy Wonka's Golden Tickets inside the wrapper, and wins a tour of the very secret Wonka factory.

Simply by being himself, the child-hero of the magic kingdom, Charlie outshines all the very spoiled children on the tour and is given the whole chocolate factory for his own. The sequel, *Charlie and the Great Glass Elevator,* continues the story of the boy's friendship with the eccentric Wonka.

In another story by Dahl, *James and the Giant Peach,* a boy harried by two awful aunts boldly escapes on the giant fruit, sails the Atlantic, and ends up in New York. The story ends with the peach pit appropriately placed next to the Alice in Wonderland statue in Central Park.

DE BRUNHOFF, JEAN
The Story of Babar, published in French, delighted *Pooh* author A. A. Milne so much that he arranged for *Babar* to appear in English. Since then, *Babar* has won friends everywhere, for the witty and unforgettable illustrations as much as for the story.

Babar, although quite his own elephant, has heroic qualities we've seen in other characters of the magic kingdom. Babar is a young elephant who travels to the strange and challenging land called Paris, where he wins the love and admiration of friends through his courtesy and natural nobility.

When he returns home all grown up, he exchanges his impeccable Parisian derby for—what else—a crown. What he has learned about himself in exotic Paris has prepared him for kingship in his own world.

You can find *Babar* in the large format, with the text in script, that you remember from your own childhood.

ENDE, MICHAEL

In *The Neverending Story,* Bastian longs to escape from life and into books, but the one he's reading challenges him in ways he never thought possible. Like Barrie's *Peter Pan, The Neverending Story* reminds us not only that we need fantasy, but that fantasy needs us, too. Ende creates a landscape of imagination worthy of its name— Fantastica—and offers a child-hero whose growth in wisdom, strength, and imagination is adventurous and exciting.

HAMILTON, VIRGINIA

Hamilton's *The People Could Fly,* beautifully illustrated by Leo and Diane Dillon, is a collection of African-American folktales. In these powerful stories, the hero is a slave who not only survives, but maintains his dignity, and gains freedom through courage, intelligence, and imagination, the qualities celebrated in the magic kingdom tradition.

The Magic Adventures of Pretty Pearl tells the story of a child in the Reconstruction era who finds a secret world deep in the woods of Georgia. Here the "inside people" live entirely apart from the troubles outside. The theme of the magic kingdom also appears in Hamilton's shorter works, *The Time-Ago Tales of Jahdu* and *Time-Ago Lost: More Tales of Jahdu.*

LE GUIN, URSULA K.

Le Guin's Earthsea trilogy—*A Wizard of Earthsea, The Tombs of Atuan,* and *The Farthest Shore*—presents a magic kingdom that reminds some readers of Tolkien's Middle-earth. The story follows the growth of a gifted young magician, Ged, as he learns the power of language and its crucial connection to identity. Your child will especially enjoy Ged's progress in an isolated school for wizards and his first experiments with his power.

LINDGREN, ASTRID

Lindgren is most widely known for her wonderfully funny character Pippi Longstocking. *Ronia, the Robber's Daughter,* explores a more dramatic story of independent girlhood. Ronia is the only child of Matt, the robber chieftain, and at a very young age this

[211]

child-hero ventures fearlessly out into the surrounding forest, whose dangers spring from imagination as well as nature. There she meets Birk, the son of a rival robber chieftain, and the two grow up in what they come to regard as their own secret forest world, a magic kingdom that they rule together. The natural and magical challenges they face together help them to win peace for their families and freedom for themselves.

NESBIT, E.

The books of E. Nesbit, especially *The Five Children and It,* were a great influence upon C. S. Lewis in his writing of the Narnia stories. Like Lewis's children, the Bastable brothers and sisters suddenly discover magic, and then find that its rules demand all their wit and spirit. Nesbit's magic is never a holiday, as the children expect. Instead, it's a challenge, a test of intellect, imagination, and courage, just as in the stories of the magic kingdom.

NORDSTROM, URSULA

In Nordstrom's *The Secret Language,* Vicky and Martha, at boarding school together, give their growing friendship a special depth by developing their own language. This is a memorable story about the challenges that face older children, becoming more independent and needing a special friend to share their growth. The secret language itself creates a world—a magic kingdom—that the girls can feel is their home, a place where they can share their secrets and their trust.

PATERSON, KATHERINE

In Paterson's *Bridge to Terabithia,* a country boy and a city girl join imaginations to make their own imaginary realm together, learning and growing through their fantasy and their friendship. Leslie and Jesse decide to stake out a part of the woods just for themselves, and name their secret land "Terabithia." It's a place, Leslie says, "like Narnia," and she lends Jesse all her Narnia books "so he would know how things went in a magic kingdom."

They both build a castle stronghold from which to rule their secret land, keeping a rope to swing on as the only bridge. It is this bridge that comes to symbolize both separation and renewal in the magic kingdom of Terabithia.

This is a very moving story, with a sad ending, and appropriate for older children who will see the role imagination has in creating a sense of ourselves and each other.

PHELPS, ETHEL JOHNSTON

Tatterhood and Other Tales and *The Maid of the North* are collections of folktales that celebrate child-heroes, all young girls, who rely on themselves and their own magic to deal with the world. Instead of being transformed or rescued by fairy godmothers, they actively work to best their challengers, in the tradition of the child-heroes of the magic kingdom.

TRAVERS, P. L.

In Travers's series, Mary Poppins magically returns again and again, with new adventures and surprises. *Mary Poppins Comes Back* tells more about the language of babies and birds, and includes a mystical reflection on the power of the newborn human child. Look for the new editions of the series, with Travers's updated revisions.

INDEX